SENSE & RESPOND

SENSE & RESPOND

*How Successful Organizations
Listen to Customers and
Create New Products
Continuously*

JEFF GOTHELF & JOSH SEIDEN

HARVARD BUSINESS REVIEW PRESS

Boston, Massachusetts

The web addresses referenced in this book were live and correct at the time of the book's publication but may be subject to change.

Library of Congress Cataloging-in-Publication Data

Names: Gothelf, Jeff, author. | Seiden, Josh, author.
  Title: Sense and respond : how successful organizations listen to customers and create new products continuously / Jeff Gothelf and Josh Seiden.
  Description: Boston, Massachusetts : Harvard Business Review Press, [2017]
  Identifiers: LCCN 2016033762 | ISBN 9781633691889 (hardcover)
  Subjects: LCSH: Organizational effectiveness. | Organizational resilience. | Customer relations–Management. | Corporate culture.
  Classification: LCC HD58.9 .G6795 2017 | DDC 658.8/12–dc23 LC record available at https://lccn.loc.gov/2016033762

The paper used in this publication meets the requirements of the American National Standard for Permanence of Paper for Publications and Documents in Libraries and Archives Z39.48-1992.

Contents

Contents

Acknowledgments

We could never have written this book without the generous support of our friends, family, coworkers, colleagues, and industry experts. We're grateful for the support we've received and would like to thank some folks in particular.

Thanks first to our editor at Harvard Business Review Press, Jeff Kehoe, and the wonderful team there who've been so helpful to us. We're particularly grateful to Stephani Finks, who designed a beautiful cover despite having two designers as clients. Thanks also to our agent, Esmond Harmsworth, for connecting us with Harvard. We owe Bruce Wexler a great deal of gratitude for helping us shape the proposal that allowed us to meet Esmond and Jeff. Thanks too to Stephen Parry for graciously sharing book titles with us.

No acknowledgment would be complete without thanking our colleagues and coworkers at Neo, from whom we learned so much. There are over a hundred of you, so we regret we can't thank you all by name. But we do love and appreciate you.

We benefitted from some generous manuscript readers down the stretch. Giff Constable and Lane Goldstone both shared tough love. Victoria Olsen was particularly incisive late in the game.

Our colleagues on the lean and agile path offered inspiration and support: Bill Scott, Eric Ries, Jeff Patton, Barry O'Reilly, Jonathan Bertfield, David Bland, and Jono Mallanyk.

We're particularly grateful to the folks working on the front lines who generously gave their time and insight during the research process to help us understand what's really happening inside organizations today. Thanks to Neil Williams, Dan North, Sonja Kresojevic, Dan Smith, Ian Muir, Rebecca Hendry, Leisa Reichelt, MJ Broadbent, Bill DeRouchey, Dave Cronin, Dan Harrelson, Greg Petroff, Bruce McCarthy, Matias Kiviniemi, Fred Santarpia, Nick Rockwell, Ines Bravo, Corinne Mayans, Stephen Orban, Scout Addis, Michele Tepper, Dan Ryan, Arpan Podduturi, Tom Griffiths, Marvin Lange, Nathan Coe, Tony Collins, Chris Kelly, Mark Chamberlain, Emily Culp, Brendan Marsh, Jez Humble, Melissa Perri, Alethea Hannemann, Matthew Hayto, Kristen Teti, Liz Hamburg, Kevin Heery, David Fine, Dagny Prieto, Hendrik Kleinsmiede, and Karen Pascoe.

And finally, thanks to our families for enduring the writing days, nights, and weekends even though we swore our previous book was our last. Carrie, Grace, and Sophie—once again, your patience and support made this book possible. Vicky, Naomi, and Amanda—you're the best.

Introduction

A Two-Way Conversation
with the Market

I n 1975, a researcher named Steven Sasson, working in a lab at Eastman Kodak, built the first digital camera. It was a clunky machine, but Sasson's vision was clear. He saw the potential: in fifteen to twenty years, he told executives, the technology would be ready to compete against film. You could hardly blame executives for their skepticism, though: the contraption needed a tape drive to operate and took nearly thirty seconds to produce a tiny, low-resolution, black-and-white image. Still, Sasson and Kodak kept at it. Indeed, by 1989, they had created a commercially viable digital camera. But Kodak executives never got behind it. In the years that followed, digital photography blossomed, but Kodak did not—or could not—respond. Digital camera sales overtook film cameras by 2004. Kodak declared bankruptcy in 2012.[1]

It's easy to see this story as a failure to innovate, and, of course, that's true in part. The lessons of *The Innovator's Dilemma* are obvious in this story: business leaders often miss the threat posed by disruptive technology until it's too late.

It would be a mistake, though, to think this story is only about innovation. It's about much more than that. We all now recognize that digital technology in its many forms is disrupting traditional businesses. Now we have to ask, What are we, as leaders, going to do about that problem? In other words, we sense the threat. Now we face a new question: How should we respond?

––––––––––

Borders, the bookstore chain, certainly sensed the threat. By 2006, Amazon.com had overtaken Borders in sales.[2] The large bricks-and-mortar retailer was struggling to respond. Borders was facing a handful of problems. Its superstore strategy, which offered an unrivaled selection of books and music to customers in the 1990s, was no longer enough to keep it ahead of its competitors: internet-based retailers could offer literally every book in print in the world, without having to support giant stores. If in-store selection was formerly its competitive advantage, that was no longer working. Borders would have to find something else. Perhaps it could compensate by building a robust online business? Yet its response to the threat of internet retailing seems, in retrospect, an obviously doomed strategy. From 2001 to 2008, Borders outsourced its internet business to Amazon.

Increasing the pressure, Amazon released its first Kindle e-reader in November 2007. The device, which was a hit from the day it was launched, opened a new front in the war on physical bookstores. Now it wasn't simply a battle between physical retail and e-commerce. Now consumers could download ebooks directly to their handheld devices. Two years later, Apple launched the iPad along with its own digital bookstore. In 2010, Barnes & Noble followed with NOOK, a product it had developed. Later that year, Borders announced a partnership with Kobo, a Canadian startup that had recently entered the e-reader space. But it was too little, too late. In 2011, Borders announced it was closing up shop for good.

Borders, it seems, didn't deny it had to respond to the digital threat. Unlike Kodak, it did respond. But Borders was never able to embrace and integrate digital capabilities and the operating methods that go with them. In other words, it just picked the wrong response.

Only the most stubborn leader would dismiss the threat posed by digital technology. Indeed, we take it as a truism that digital technology is here to stay. It has (for better and for worse) reshaped our world, and the world in which we do business. It has put mighty incumbents out of business and has created a generation of newly mighty companies.

But the economy has changed, too. It's not just the presence of technology. Instead, what has changed is the new things that people are doing as a result of technology. People now have remarkable new capabilities to communicate with one another—both directly and indirectly—and with the organizations that serve their interests. People can share personal messages with friends, groups, and strangers around the world. People can share their opinions of a merchant's products by posting online reviews. And the organizations serving these people's needs also can take advantage of these rich communication channels. They can see almost immediately how their products are performing online. What's selling? What are people saying about them? What features are working? What's not working?

Savvy companies are taking advantage of this new communication capability. They continuously try new things in the market, testing and rapidly adjusting based on what they learn. In the mid-2000s, Spanish retailer Zara became well known for its so-called fast fashion approach, an approach made possible by digital technology. Zara produces as many as ten thousand designs annually, many of which live for a very short time. It produces the designs in small numbers, observes what works, rapidly communicates back to design centers, and adjusts based on what it has learned. Customers may not know that they're providing feedback, but they're voting with their wallets, and the company treats that information as its lifeblood.[3]

In a more purely digital realm, Google has become the dominant search engine in part because it has leveraged the power of running continuous small experiments to optimize its service. Some experts estimate that Google may run more than thirty thousand experiments a year to improve its search product. If you've used Google (and who hasn't?), then, in all likelihood, you've participated in many of these experiments.[4]

You can think of both the Zara story and the Google story as being about the same thing: companies engaging in what we call a *two-way conversation with the market*. Companies that formerly moved at an annual pace can try new things, learn from their customer interactions, and adjust their plans quickly. In response, customers see new offerings from companies, vote with their wallets, and express their feelings with their reviews, their tweets, their Facebook posts, and their YouTube videos. All this happens incredibly quickly. And the speed and richness of this conversation are putting fundamental pressure on businesses, governments, and other institutions: they must change the way they respond to the market, or go the way of Kodak, Borders, and a long list of others.

In this book, we talk about digital technology, but digital technology—software—is simply the enabler for this two-way conversation with the market, this new way of operating in the world. The real subject of this book is the way management must change to deal with this conversation.

The problem that many of us face is that most of our management techniques were created at a time when this two-way conversation didn't exist. Instead, our management tools were built for a completely different pace of operations—the pace of the past century's manufacturing economy. Operations in the manufacturing age were slower and more predictable. They rewarded a management approach based on planning, deliberation, and secrecy. The economies of scale in a manufacturing economy made it difficult to change plans in midstream, but there was less need to change plans in that era. Adjustments made on an annual basis were sufficient.

That is no longer true. Imagine a website that is updated only once a year: it's an absurd scenario. When your customers can have a new version of your product in their hands every day, why would you wait a year to respond to feedback? Why would they tolerate that? Now imagine this scenario multiplied across all of your customers, partners, and workers—indeed all the players in our economy. Imagine this scenario applied to the software and policies that are used to operate your business, your supply chain, your distribution. This is the situation we face. Increasingly, the relationship with our partners is dominated by the two-way conversation that digital technology allows. In the face of this new pace and these new expectations, our management systems—built for the manufacturing economy that dominated in the past century—are worse than insufficient. They are failing badly. They are in need of an update.

The Two-Way Conversation
Requires a Management Shift

Often, we fail to make a fundamental reassessment of the way we manage our business as a whole in the era of digital technology. Instead, the standard response within existing organizations has been to create a stand-alone or outsourced information technology (IT) capability.

This is a legacy not only of how we think about technology but also of how we think about and structure our organizations, a legacy we inherited from the very successful innovations of the past century: Henry Ford's assembly line, Taylor's scientific management principles, and the engineering model of organizations. This legacy of functional segregation in the name of efficiency makes sense in certain contexts, but unfortunately it doesn't work in the digital reality. The complexity of software systems, the challenge of predicting what the market wants, the pace of change within the market itself— all this stacks the odds against these stand-alone approaches.

When Borders outsourced its internet bookstore to Amazon, it did more than relinquish control of this channel to a competitor. It robbed itself of a crucial opportunity to have a two-way conversation with this emerging customer segment, to engage with this new type of customer behavior, to learn what the customer wanted, and to learn how to serve that customer online. Never mind that Borders didn't know how to run an e-commerce business in 2001; almost no one did back then. Indeed, you could argue that Amazon barely knew how to do it back then. Instead, from 2001 to 2008, Borders gave Amazon an opportunity to learn, on the Borders nickel, and with Borders customers, how to win—and all because it allowed

Amazon to sit in the middle of a conversation Borders should have been having directly with its own customers.

The new playbook emerging from the technology industry gives us the ability to integrate this two-way conversation deep within the fabric of our organizations. Let's take a moment to look at this playbook and consider why it relevant to us.

Agile: A Playbook for the Information Age

The first people to seek out a new playbook were software engineers working in the 1980s and 1990s. A handful of frustrated and thoughtful practitioners looked at the software development process and asked why, at the time, it seemed difficult to create effective software systems. (Looking back on that moment, it's easy to see why there was so much frustration. A well-known study from that period—*The CHAOS Report (1994),* by The Standish Group—found that 84 percent of IT projects either failed to deliver *any* results or were seriously impaired by cost and schedule overruns.) These practitioners concluded that the methods we had been using to make software until that point were based on the wrong model.

The software development models that were dominant at the time were based on the time-honored process models of the past century. But they were based on building things like cars and buildings. Things that had concrete and easily understood requirements. Things with stresses and loads and other properties that could be calculated with proven equations. Things that you could figure out in great detail prior to manufacturing, and then create plans that you could hand off to builders. Plans that didn't change after the assembly process started.

Our group of frustrated practitioners realized the key difference in working with software: requirements always seemed to change after the project got started. For years, programmers fought this battle by fighting against requirements changes. But this group took a different approach. They asked, What if we embraced change? What if, for whatever reason, changing requirements are an inevitable part of the software development process, and what if we optimized our process for change?

If you've been close to the digital technology world, you'll recognize that question as the seed of what eventually grew into the *agile movement*. Once a kind of counterculture insurgency, agile is now mainstream and is on its way to becoming the dominant process model for software development.

Agile embraces change in a variety of ways, but at its core, it uses two techniques. First, it breaks the work into small batch sizes, and, second, it uses continuous market feedback to guide progress. So unlike an assembly line—where the customer doesn't see the car until the product is completely through the line—in an agile process, a small unit of software is made and presented to a user, feedback is collected, and, based on that feedback, the team decides what next steps to take. Perhaps the team continues as planned. Perhaps the team adjusts its priorities. Perhaps the team designs something new. The ability to create a continuous feedback cycle is the most important thing we gain as our economy moves from the manufacture of hard goods to the production of software and the delivery of services built on top of software. This feedback loop allows us to build learning into our daily operating rhythm.

The implications of this change in process are profound. Now teams are not working strictly to a preset plan. Instead, they use the feedback loop to learn their way forward. They can't promise that they'll produce a Model T at a specific time. Instead, they decide what to build as they are in the process of building it.

Sense and Respond

When you look at the methods that have been developed in the past twenty-five years in the software world, you'll see that many of the most influential ideas share the agile concept of a continuous feedback loop—this notion of a continuous conversation with the market—whether it's designers bringing the ideas of user-centered design, design thinking, and lean UX, entrepreneurs like Eric Ries and Steve Blank bringing lean startup and customer development, or technologists bringing lean and agile methods and DevOps practices.

More than that, though, we've seen the way these new methods for engaging the market have led to new leadership approaches. The authors of this book have worked in the technology industry for many years. We've watched and participated in the development of these methods, and we're excited to report on them to you. We've seen an entire industry form and a body of knowledge start to collect about working in ways that create a two-way conversation with the market, and we're excited to share what we've learned with you. As you'll see, we believe these methods apply far beyond technology's borders.

We've named this book *Sense and Respond* because we like the way this phrase describes the basic mechanism, the feedback loop, at the center of this approach. The most important themes that underpin the sense and respond approach can be found in these five key principles.

> *Create two-way conversations.* Digital technology has given us the new ability to have two-way conversations with our

markets and our customers. What does the market want? And by *market* here, we mean *people*. (When we talk about being user centered, customer centered, and human centered, we're referring to this idea.) Understanding the unexpressed and unmet needs of the people who are using our products, services, and technology is the key to unlocking value. In this ability is the key to success in the digital age: we don't have to predict what will work. Instead, we can listen, make a credible guess, get feedback in nearly real time, and adjust.

Focus on the outcomes. In the digital age, it's difficult, and sometimes impossible, to predict which product features are needed in the market. Yet often, we plan our features and manage our business cycles as if we know exactly what's going to work. We manage by specifying outputs—what we'll make. Instead, we need to focus on outcomes: management needs to declare the business outcomes they wish to achieve and then set up their teams to figure out how to get there. This means that we have to create the conditions in which teams can try different approaches, experiment, learn, and discover what works through trial and error.

Embrace continuous change and continuous processes. Modern digital development practices allow teams to make small changes in an ongoing way. This allows them to make the adjustments they need to make when they're using a sense and respond approach. But it also changes how we plan, because we're continuously learning and adjusting our plans as we go. And it changes how we budget, because we can no longer afford to make commitments a year in advance when we're learning every day. And it changes how we market, and sell, and . . . so much more. We have to move away from big-batch manufacturing processes and adopt small-batch, continuous processes.

Create collaboration. All great digital efforts are collaborations—between a creator and the audience. Between developers and operations people. Between designers and business stakeholders. You need to embrace collaboration deeply and break down walls where you find them. This means that we need to consider how we organize our teams, our departments, our programs, and our initiatives.

Create a learning culture. Sense and respond means embracing a way of working that is about continuous learning, which requires significant changes to process and organizational structures. This need to change, in turn, means we must build a learning culture, and that requires openness, humility, and permission to fail. It means supporting curiosity and collaboration. It means having a willingness to admit we don't really know the answer and an eagerness to go find it. Finally, it means embracing change and embracing the idea that software is a continuous, mutable medium.

Why This Book?

The management playbook that is emerging in the technology world has much to offer the larger business leadership community. This playbook enables organizations to engage in the two-way conversation with the market and to drive value from that conversation.

The product teams in technology-centered companies tend to work in a continuous small-batch rhythm, creating small product updates, sensing the performance of the product, and responding continuously with adjustments. Some of these adjustments take the form of new software—but not always. Sometimes the adjustments are to business rules, or pricing, or marketing language, or support policies, or any of the many other variables that go into running a successful business. Regardless of the adjustment, though, the teams focus on creating outcomes, shun detailed feature road maps, and are guided by the continuous conversation with the market.

We wrote about these emerging principles in our first book, *Lean UX*, which describes a work system based on small, collaborative teams that deliver value rapidly and continuously. Though written for a technical audience, the book offers a state-of-the-art model for working with digital technology that applies to everyone. These new-model teams are the engine at the heart of business today.

As we traveled the world teaching these methods to practitioners, though, we kept hearing one constant theme. "We'd love to work this way," they said, "but it's so hard in this organization." And as we dug deeper into their concerns, we saw a common pattern. The organizations in which they worked were not set up to support this new way of working.

Large organizations work in the opposite way: creating detailed plans and pushing them down to an execution factory—a staff of order takers. Large organizations tend to behave like a production line, outsourcing execution and isolating decision making within the higher levels. Instead of a conversation, these organizations are simply pushing "Play" on a prerecorded speech.

What You'll Find in This Book

Part I explains the sense and respond model: why it's so important, how it works, when to use it (and when not to), what obstacles you're likely to face, and how to overcome them.

Part II is our manager's guide to sense and respond. It explains how to adjust your teams and your planning processes to work in this way, how to experiment to unlock value, and how to structure your operations for continuous, predictable delivery. Our goal is not to teach every manager all the intricacies of each technique (there are lots of great books that focus on individual tactics) but instead to give managers an overview of the important techniques, explaining how they work together and why they are such important parts of the system.

The Power of Sense and Respond

As we've worked with organizations over the past few years to imagine, design, build, and launch new products and services that incorporate digital technology, we've seen the power of the sense and respond approach—and the necessity of building it in to your organization. We're seeing that leading organizations have started this evolution and are accelerating as a result. The small startup teams that have no legacy organizational baggage are adopting these techniques as the natural order of things, and they too are leaving their mark on the world. We think the ideas in this book—simple, practical ideas that don't require you to be a technologist—are critical for any manager, and that is why we're eager to share them with you.

And, because we also use the sense and respond approach ourselves, we want to hear your feedback. So please, as you read, keep
in mind that we too are open to a two-way conversation. So that
you can continue your learning journey, we've created an online
companion site to this book. You can find all the source material
we reference in this book at http://senseandrespond.co/links/. If you
want to get in touch with us directly, you can write to us at josh@
joshuaseiden.com and jeff@jeffgothelf.com. Let us know what you
think. Let us know how this approach works in your organization,
for your team, and for your products and services. We'd love to hear
from you.

The Sense and Respond Model

1

Continuous Uncertainty

Everything's Changing, All the Time

I t was Christmas 2012, and Facebook was more popular than ever before. What's more, smartphones and digital photography were more ubiquitous than ever before, and Facebook was far and away the most popular photo uploading destination. But with all these photo uploads came a new problem for the social networking site: people were reporting millions of photos as inappropriate. To review all these reported photos in a timely fashion would have taken thousands of people.

This story, first reported by NPR in 2015, caught the attention of mainstream readers.[1] But the tech world has heard stories like it before. Increasingly, it is the new normal for companies working in the digital space: companies launch software, the software has unpredictable effects, and companies struggle to respond. That's because the digital revolution has brought to the world of business two critical forces. The first is uncertainty: as our software systems get more complex, it becomes harder to predict what people will do with them. Savvy companies are adapting their processes to deal with this by harnessing the second force: continuous change. Unlike manufacturing products, digital products can be changed and updated rapidly. Organizations that apply the power of continuous change to products, services, and their businesses as a whole are able to adapt quickly in the face of uncertainty.

Older methods for dealing with uncertainty don't work in the digital age. Careful, detailed planning, for example, fails over and over. In 2013 the British Broadcasting Corporation shut down a decade-long attempt to build a new, organization-wide content management system. The project, called the Digital Media Initiative, was supposed to allow BBC staff to create, share, and manage digital content from their desktops. Despite the careful plans made by the project team and sponsors, after many years and close to £100 million, the project had delivered no value. Project managers complained that requirements kept changing, making it impossible for them to deliver. In other words, no matter how diligently they planned, the plans never worked. Conditions kept changing. The BBC project failed.

Every business leader you speak to can probably tell you similar stories of software-related projects and strategic initiatives that failed to deliver value, failed to deliver on budget, failed to deliver on time, or simply failed to deliver. Every year, our society wastes hundreds of billions of dollars on failed software efforts, mostly because we think we can use industrial-age management approaches on digital-age problems.

At the same time, software has become an ever more critical building block for every business of any significant size. At Goldman Sachs, for example, the largest single division in the firm is now technology, employing eight thousand—a full 25 percent—of the firm's thirty-two thousand employees.

Slowly but surely, we watch as the products and services around us are transformed by software. Apple's iPhone spelled doom for

Nokia and RIM, two companies that were built on technological excellence but couldn't cope with the unpredictable change wrought by the software revolution. Amazon did the same to Borders and Barnes & Noble. Netflix did it to Blockbuster.

The software revolution is here, and we can't predict the ways it will play out. Customers use products in unpredictable ways. Competitors emerge where we least expect them. This new level of volatility and uncertainty is one of the side effects of the digital revolution. We need new ways to respond.

———————

The team at Facebook could have simply hired more reviewers to deal with the deluge of "inappropriate" photos, but before it did, it started to look into the reported photos. That's when the Facebook team discovered something strange: most of the photos were not actually inappropriate. There were photos of people in ugly sweaters, people hanging out with their ex-boyfriends and ex-girlfriends, people in unflattering poses. The photos weren't inappropriate—no nudity, no harassment, no drug use, no hate speech. But Facebook's photo reporting tool didn't have an "ugly sweater" category, so if you didn't like a photo of yourself, you had little choice: you had to report it as something, and "inappropriate" seemed to be the best option.

This is uncertainty at work. Users come to a system with an idea of what they're trying to do. If they don't see an easy way to do it, they'll try to find a way. Just as a stream flows around obstacles, cutting unpredictable paths along the way, so will a group of users find the easiest, fastest ways to achieve their goal. If they can find a way to do it on your system, they will, even if it means doing something you hadn't predicted, like reporting an unflattering photo as inappropriate. And if they can't find a way to do what they want to do, they're likely to abandon your service in favor of something better.

Facebook's product team responded by trying to fix the reporting feature—and it used what we call a *sense and respond* approach to dealing with uncertainty. Because team members weren't sure what was going on, they started to update the product in a way that would help them figure it out. First, they added a new step to the reporting process—a question that asked, "Why are you reporting this photo?" This open-ended question helped them learn that, in most cases, people were embarrassed by the photos they were reporting. Armed with this knowledge, the team updated the product again, this time asking people to contact the poster in these cases of embarrassing photos. This helped but didn't solve the problem.

Then the Facebook team added a blank message box so that people could use the reporting feature to contact the poster directly. The team tested that. It was a little better. Then it added a default message in the message box. That was better still. The team members tried lots of different small changes, pushing these changes out to small segments of the user population. Each time, the changes attempted both to fix the problem and to get more information about the problem.

Eventually, by tweaking and trying and asking and measuring, the team was able to solve the problem. The reporting feature now has a category for embarrassing photos, directs users to contact the person who posted the photo, and prompts the poster with a carefully tested written message (which users can edit but rarely do).

Still, if you now go to Facebook and report a photo, there's a good chance you'll see something different from what we've described here. That's because somewhere at Facebook, someone is probably looking at the numbers on this feature, spotting a problem, and running tests to improve the situation. This is sense and respond, and it's a continuous process.

Facing Uncertainty

The uncertainties faced by the team at Facebook are the new normal. The tactics the team deployed are the emerging standard for how to respond. And even though the tactics can be thought of as simply a management approach (measure customer behavior, test solutions, scale what works), they rely on the ability to act, and act quickly. Until now, the common response in business and government has been to consider technology the domain of specialists and segregate it from core business operations. We know now that this approach doesn't work. The reason it doesn't work is that it reduces the business's capability to act.

In other words, we no longer have the luxury of ignoring technology—or leaving it to the technologists. Instead, we must all become adept at managing in the face of it—both the uncertainty it creates and opportunities it offers. The reality is this: assigning responsibility for software to your IT department is like assigning responsibility for breathing to an oxygen department.

Seeing the End of Assembly Line Management

To understand why we advocate changing the way we run our organizations, we need to take a step back and consider what's changed. Much of the management science that we take for granted was developed for the production of a certain kind of product. As production has changed—we're making different things in new ways from new materials—so too does our management approach need to change.

We all know the story of Henry Ford and the assembly line: by breaking down predictable, repetitive work into small, repeatable pieces, Ford was able to revolutionize manufacturing, establish the dominant position in the auto industry, and change the way businesses around the world thought about the production of material goods. This model created tremendous value and wealth and stands as the dominant model for the way we think about business.

Our early introduction to personal computer technology and software offered little evidence that computers and software were different from cars—or from any of the other modern engineered products we create with an assembly line approach. Certainly the laptops and phones and other high-tech devices we buy are made on assembly lines—very advanced assembly lines to be sure, but assembly lines nevertheless. And the first software programs consumers purchased seemed to be like any other product. We walked into the computer store, picked up a big shrink-wrapped box of Microsoft Office or Lotus 1-2-3, and took it home to install it. These products certainly appeared to be "manufactured" products, even if the software developers of the time suspected that something was different.

But with the first wave of internet companies in the late 1990s, we began to see a new kind of software distribution model emerge: software as a service (SaaS). In this model, we didn't install software on our local computers. Instead, the software ran on a company's server, and we consumed it over the web, in our browsers. One of the values that SaaS companies promised was that you'd never need to go to the store or install a software update again; the latest version of the software would always be available to you, because it would always be running on the company's servers.

Escaping the Manufacturing Mindset

This shift may seem like a small process change, but it's hard to overstate how significant a paradigm shift it represents. Why? It's because the manufacturing process—the process of copying software onto floppy disks or CDs or DVDs—is no longer part of the software distribution process. And by removing this one step, we've enabled a fundamentally new model.

In this new model, the conversation with customers changes: you no longer have to convince them to buy a new version. You just push it to your server. You no longer have to convince them to install an upgrade; they see it when they log on.

The new model changes the economic incentives, too. In industries that are built around mass manufacturing, the high cost of launching new products is defrayed by the efficiency of the assembly line, so the natural incentive is to set up your production lines once and then crank out as many units as possible. Automakers created a well-known annual "model year" product cycle to take advantage of this while still meeting the market's need for new products. This annual rhythm is so ingrained in us it almost appears to be a natural phenomenon, but it's not: it's a strategy based on the way products are produced.

Consider this stunning fact: Amazon releases new software to the world every 11.6 seconds.[2] This is possible because of a set of techniques called *continuous deployment*. Basically, continuous deployment allows software developers to keep systems in a constant state of readiness and to make incremental changes to those systems in an ongoing way. Amazon is one of the leaders here, but it's becoming routine for large companies to release software daily, and, for many companies, we see releases multiple times a day.

What does this mean for managers? We think it's not an exaggeration to say that it changes everything. In the digital world, there is no longer any "manufacturing." In a world with a manufacturing step, the cost of change is high; every time you make a change to the product, you need to go through manufacturing again, and that incurs costs. So there's an incentive to limit how often we change our manufactured goods. Without that process step, though, we remove that constraint. Instead, the constraints on change exist elsewhere in the system—how much change a customer can tolerate, for instance, or how much change we can make without reducing quality or increasing other costs. But as industry leaders like Amazon are demonstrating, these constraints are much less restrictive than we might imagine. In practice, it is now possible to present new features, capabilities, and services to our customers and our internal staff on a continuous basis and at a remarkably rapid pace.

Finding Value in Uncertainty

Why does Amazon release software so often? It's not only because it can do it. No, instead, releasing software frequently is only one element in the sense and respond approach. This approach to work involves rapid cycles of *sensing* what the market needs and *responding* rapidly. As you saw in the Facebook story, this approach allows teams to make sense of complexity, reduce uncertainty, and find solutions that work.

Let's look at some of the benefits of working this way.

Delivering Services

The first generation of consumer software changed how we work. Spreadsheets and word processors created a boom in personal productivity. But first-generation software was also inflexible. This meant that when organizations tried to deliver services through software, the result was often terrible. Inefficient. Confusing. Hard to use.

Picture yourself calling a call center, perhaps to talk about your phone bill. How many times have you heard the call-center operator struggling with her computer system? In the past, business processes and customer behavior often had to adapt to the way the software worked, because the rate at which we could change software was slow. We once overheard a group of industrial plastics executives comparing benchmarks on their customer-service process. They were talking about how many orders each business processed each day. The average seemed to be about thirty orders a day. Then one executive spoke up: "We used to process about thirty a day. Then we installed a new order-taking system. We're doing about two a day now."

With our new ability to change software on a continuous basis, businesses have a new ability to deliver customer services that are based on, mediated by, or simply supported with software. Software, which can be inflexible, is only now living up to its potential to be "soft," and this process flexibility gives us new overall flexibility when it comes to delivering services to the market. Whereas formerly we'd roll out a service and be stuck with it, now we can roll it out and adjust it until it works properly. And if we need to change a policy or process, we can adjust the software that supports it nearly as easily.

Reducing Risk

If you've followed the news, you've heard about massive technology projects that fail. A recent headline on CIO.com was blunt: "Enterprise software project success remains elusive."[3] Industry analysts at The Standish Group, who study technology project outcomes, have been benchmarking the industry for years. Their most recent study puts IT failure rates at around 70 percent, a number that is better than the more than 80 percent failure rates of the 1990s, but still.

In Massachusetts, for example, the state government spent more than nineteen years and more than $75 million on a system to connect the state's courthouses to one another. It was supposed to take five years. After nineteen years, though, most observers consider the project unfinished and useless: a very expensive failure.

Sense and respond methods can help this. Traditional IT projects tend to take a "big bang" approach, in which the software is not released to users until it is finished. This means that it's hard to tell whether the team building the system is on the right track until the end of the project. In contrast, an agile approach, which is at the heart of sense and respond, would address this problem by releasing small pieces of the system frequently and would do so from the earliest days of the project. This reduces the risk that the software team is off course, because it creates transparency. It becomes easy to see what the team is doing, because it's sharing its work continuously.

This transparency is key because it enables a feedback loop. Is the software working? Is it meeting user needs? Is it creating the outcomes the business seeks? Why wait until the end of the project to find out?

Optimizing for Value

Imagine for a moment that you're an executive at Amazon. You run a huge e-commerce business, and you make money when people buy things from you. To buy things from you, people must complete the checkout process on your website. Thus, it is in your interest to optimize the checkout flow so that people can navigate through it with great success. You don't want to confuse people. You don't want to distract people. You want them to move through the flow until they complete the transaction.

One technique that Amazon and similar companies use to optimize the process very quickly is to release different versions of a portion of their website—for example, the checkout flow—and route incoming traffic to the variant versions, comparing the performance of the versions. This is the scientific method in action. It's called *A/B testing,* and it's become a standard technique in the online world. For example, this technique was what the team at Facebook used to test its solutions to the photo-reporting problem. Companies like Amazon perform many tests every day in an ongoing effort to optimize their flows. And even though it may not seem that these optimizations could be very valuable, in fact the opposite is true. In one well-known case, a large online retailer unlocked $300 million in annual sales by changing the wording on *one button* in the checkout flow.[4]

In 2012, the Obama campaign used this technique on nearly everything it launched on its campaign website. In one case, the team was trying to optimize the donation page. Team members tried many variations before they decided to try adding a simple quote from the president to the page. Compared with the page without the quote, this page generated an 11.6 percent increase in donations. That may not seem like much, but given its volume, that simple change increased donations by millions of dollars over the life of the campaign.[5]

This approach to optimization is enabled by two important factors. First, you need the technical infrastructure in place to run these tests, gather the results, and route the results quickly to the right people. More important is the second factor: management attitude. Managers need to be able to admit that they don't have all the answers, and they must be willing, in the right circumstances, to submit their ideas to testing in the marketplace. This new management mindset is only the first of the important management innovations we need to adopt if businesses are going to succeed in the digital age.

Recognizing Emergent Value

To understand what we call "emergent value," we need to step back and consider the nature of the products and services that technology is now making possible.

In the early days of the computer revolution, when the first personal computers were coming onto the market, people talked about the "killer app"—an application that would be so useful and so compelling that it would drive large-scale purchase of these machines. It is common wisdom to claim that the spreadsheet—VisiCalc first, and then Lotus 1-2-3—was the driving force behind most early purchases of PCs. For others, the killer app was the word processor. But in either case, the uses that these programs enabled were similar: one person, sitting at one computer, interacting with the software and unlocking more productivity by means of a more efficient tool.

Think now about the killer app of our contemporary age. Imagine for a moment a computer without internet connectivity. Or even worse, imagine your smartphone in airplane mode. Without connectivity, our devices are nearly useless—they lose most of their value. This is because increasingly, our technology systems are connecting us to services and, more important, to *other people* on the internet. We use Twitter and Facebook to share news and information. We use Amazon to shop. We use Uber to summon service providers. We use Google Maps and Waze to navigate, with real-time traffic information collected by other users of the system. Our "apps" are no longer stand-alone programs running on our personal computers.

And it's not just that our users are doing new things with this connected technology. Businesses are increasingly delivering their core services through connected technology. Simple Bank, for example, is a bank that is available only through software, even though there are real humans operating the business behind the scenes. Weight

Watchers now supplements its traditional channels by allowing clients to connect to a weight-loss coach through a smartphone app.

Designing and building these new kinds of systems require a different management approach. When you start to connect apps into larger communication systems, you start to see an explosion in the level of complexity and therefore the level of uncertainty. It is difficult to predict how groups of people will use systems and, as a result, what parts of the system they will find valuable.

Consider the hashtag. This ubiquitous means of tagging content and conversations on the internet emerged from Twitter users in 2007 as a way to track their conversations with one another. This feature wasn't planned or introduced by Twitter. Rather, users of the system started to tag their conversations with keywords, which they set off by means of a leading "#" (hash) symbol. This method proved popular with users, because they could agree on a tag and then use the regular Twitter search feature to find all the tweets with that tag. In other words, it added value, and its use spread. It wasn't until two years later, in 2009, that Twitter responded by building features into the system that specifically supported the hashtag. Twitter automatically hyperlinked all tags, and clicking on that link returned a search result for that tag.[6] Now Twitter has turned the hashtag into a revenue-generating product: you can buy ads that use specific hashtags to target audiences.

The hashtag story is an example of a company responding (albeit slowly) to unpredicted user behavior in a way that captures and creates value. In this story you see the connection between user value and business value. When we can understand the things that users want to do, we have the basis for serving customer needs, thus creating business value.

But companies that are not prepared to take advantage of unpredicted user behavior run into big problems. In the BBC Digital Media Initiative example we mentioned earlier, technology managers complained that one reason for the project's failure was that internal users continually changed the system requirements. You hear this frequently in the technology world—and people make this claim as a way of pointing fingers, either at users for being fickle or at technologists for not being responsive to change. The reality is more subtle. Although careful study and analysis of user needs is important and valuable, it's not always enough. Often, requirements *cannot* be known in advance, and once a system is in use, new needs are discovered, creating new requirements.

Again, this is uncertainty at work. As the hashtag story illustrates, if businesses are open to uncertainty, they can find new ideas in the unpredicted user behaviors that emerge from uncertain situations. If they can respond appropriately, this phenomenon—emergent behavior—becomes emergent value. On the other hand, when businesses try to predict the future and reject the emergent reality, the gap between plans and reality is likely to lead to disappointment, finger-pointing, delay, and project failure.

Responding appropriately is not easy, though. It requires managers to adopt a new mindset and to be willing to adjust plans in response to new information. This new mindset embraces continuous change and uncertainty, seeks market feedback, and is willing to look within that feedback for opportunities to create new value. In short, it requires leaders to say, "I don't know the answer. Let's go find out together."

Adapting to a Complex Context

For the typical twentieth-century leader, "I don't know" was a taboo. To admit uncertainty—to oneself or others—was seen as a sign of weakness. This mindset remains common in many organizations, and it is especially a problem when it comes to seeking emergent value in *complex adaptive systems*: systems with lots of components that behave and interact in such a way as to make prediction impossible. In our context, they are systems in which it's impossible to predict accurately how people will interact with them and what features users will embrace.

Writing in *Harvard Business Review*, David Snowden and Mary E. Boone describe how these systems are different from the mechanical systems of the industrial age.

> It's like the difference between, say, a Ferrari and the Bra-zilian rainforest. Ferraris are complicated machines, but an expert mechanic can take one apart and reassemble it without changing a thing. The car is static, and the whole is the sum of its parts. The rainforest, on the other hand, is in constant flux—a species becomes extinct, weather patterns change, an agricultural project reroutes a water source—and the whole is far more than the sum of its parts. This is the realm of "unknown unknowns," and it is the domain to which much of contemporary business has shifted.[7]

Without embracing uncertainty, you can't capitalize on the value that emerges from these systems. This is why many organizations are moving toward the continuous, small, rapid, experiment-and-adjust cycle that is at the heart of the sense and respond approach. By making small, continuous changes and measuring the results, teams have discovered in practice exactly the method that complexity theorists recommend for dealing with these complex contexts.

Comparing the Old Model Versus Sense and Respond

When the digital revolution began, bringing with it new levels of complexity and uncertainty, most businesses tried to manage it using the industrial-age techniques that had worked well until then. We thought of software as just a type of Ferrari, to use Snowden and Boone's analogy. We didn't change the methods we used to make it, and we certainly didn't consider changing the way we ran our businesses to accommodate its impact.

As we've grown more sophisticated about software, though, we've learned better how to manage it. Our approaches—the agile methods that have become ubiquitous—have allowed us to treat software more like a rainforest. Our software management process is more like forestry than engineering.

Now we're ready to take the next step. As we realize the increasing reliance we place on software systems and the deep ways that the digital revolution has connected our businesses to the rest of the world through those systems, we must now begin to manage our businesses with the techniques we apply to software. In other words, where we once managed software in the same way we ran our businesses, now we need to manage our businesses in the same way we manage our software.

Understanding the Continuous Rhythm of Self-Directed Teams

In order to operate in this new, continuous rhythm, teams must be free to act. They must be free to experiment and learn. This means that teams need to be given greater decision-making authority. The assembly line approach of the industrial era sought to separate thinking (the realm of management) from doing (the realm of the worker). It tried to turn workers into assembly line machines. But people are not machines—and the process of sensing market need and responding quickly is not as conducive to similar thought- and decision-minimizing approaches. Decisions that can be made in a top-down, hierarchical manner and with predictable, measured work flow are fewer in this new world. Instead, many more decisions need to be made from the bottom up, by the people with the expertise to work with the material and with access to the most recent information. These people are the ones closest to the market, and not closest to the top of the organization.

For example, let's consider Etsy, a ten-year-old e-commerce startup based in New York. Etsy is a marketplace where buyers can purchase handcrafted goods from more than a million independent sellers; think of it as the world's largest online crafts fair. Etsy is famous for its culture of continuous experimentation. Etsy continuously tests and optimizes the design of its website and mobile apps through the A/B testing process we described earlier. It develops multiple versions of a feature, releases the various versions of that feature for a short period to a small (but carefully selected) number of users, and then monitors the results. Its sophisticated systems allow Etsy to roll back designs that are not successful, and roll out successful changes beyond the original test group. And all this happens very quickly. Using continuous deployment techniques—many of which it invented—Etsy is able to make many small changes to its website in an ongoing way, typically at a rate of forty to fifty times each day. Etsy is also famous for its decentralized culture. Each team, acting within strategic guidelines, is free to experiment, learn, and adjust.

Etsy is a software-only startup of about eight hundred people, with revenues of about $275 million per year on total merchandise sales of about $2 billion.[8] So even though its use of these techniques is impressive, it's a digital-native company. What about a more traditional industry?

Running an Auto Company Like a Software Company

Since we've been talking about Henry Ford's assembly lines, let's look at the auto industry, which is steadily being revolutionized by digital technology.

In March 2015, Tesla Motors, upstart producer of electric cars, announced that it would be solving one of its biggest obstacles to success, a problem it calls "range-anxiety": the fear that an electric car will run out of power somewhere, with no charging station within range. Elon Musk, founder of the company, promised to announce a new feature that would solve this significant need.

For about a week, the press and curious observers buzzed: How would Tesla solve the problem? Then, at a press conference, Musk revealed the solution, a new feature called "range assurance." The feature would monitor energy use and driving conditions in real time (how fast were you going? what was the weather like? was the road flat or hilly?) to continuously predict remaining range. At the same time, the feature would monitor the location of the nearest charging station. With this capability, when you reached the point of needing a charge, the car would alert you and guide you to the most appropriate charging station. You'd never run out of power, Musk said, unless you did it on purpose.

Perhaps feeling that this seemed like a small win for future models, reporters asked when this capability would be available. Musk's reply? Every current owner would receive the update shortly after the press conference—an update to their current cars—via software that would be distributed via the internet and installed in Teslas over Wi-Fi.

Moments after the press conference was over, *Consumer Reports* responded over Twitter:

> Biggest takeaway from @TeslaMotors announcement is the reminder that cars can be made to improve over time, like other electronic devices.[9]

In other words, in the same way that we now update our smartphones and our computers, we are starting to see self-updating cars. And other traditional manufactured good are likely to be next.

Changing More Than Products

We take for granted that products are becoming more sophisticated every day, so perhaps it's not surprising that Tesla cars are becoming more sophisticated. But this example is not simply about a smarter product; other dimensions of the auto industry are changing as well. These cars don't need to go to a dealership or a mechanic for an upgrade—Tesla can send out the upgrade over the wireless internet—so the process of maintenance is changed. Tesla also monitors a car's use over time, so it knows when the car needs service.

So software is changing our products—in this case the car—and it's changing the maintenance process. Anything else? Yes—it's also changing the basic release cycle of the auto industry. No longer do you need to buy next year's model to take advantage of the latest features. Instead, manufacturers can release new features whenever they are ready.

Building Hardware Products as If They're Software Products

One extreme example of this new ability to release products quickly comes to us from Chinese phone maker Xiaomi. Founded in 2010, Xiaomi releases phones in small batches—100,000 every Tuesday—and each batch sells out quickly. More impressive is this: Xiaomi continuously updates its products in response to user feedback collected on online forums. So an idea that a customer suggests can go from forum to product manager to engineer to release in a matter of days. Once again, this is a company engaging in a two-way conversation with customers.

This ability to release small batches of product with the most recent, most desirable features gives Xiaomi a huge competitive advantage. It gets immediate feedback on what the market wants, instead of having to guess. In the manufacturing world, guessing wrong can very expensive if it results in filling a warehouse with inventory that no one wants to buy. Because digital technology allows the company to both collect feedback and produce phones in small batches, it limits the risk of producing unneeded inventory. If you've been involved in retail, you know the challenges involved in forecasting production, and the cost of guessing wrong. By using tactics taken from the digital world, Xiaomi is able to limit the uncertainty of long-term forecasts, produce small batches of products, and create a high degree of certainty that it's making exactly the product the customer wants—in other words, that the product will sell.

Learning New Roles, New Methods, New Activities

In each of these cases, from Etsy to Tesla to Xiaomi, we see teams that are using the real-time capability that digital technology provides to have a two-way conversation with the market—to sense and respond. They sense which customers need attention and service. Based on what they sense, they decide which features to release or what business processes to adjust. The data they collect is powerful, but it's also disruptive: it has the effect of trumping plans, road maps, and schedules. When you have real-time information about an engine that requires service, aren't you going to prioritize that data over a planned service schedule? When you discover a market need, such as range anxiety, that is a serious problem for your customers, why would you wait until next year to solve the problem when you can fix it tomorrow?

On the other hand, you also have new problems now. How can you build a marketing campaign around exciting new features if you don't know when those features are coming—or even what features are coming in the first place? How can you write contracts for your customers if you're not sure what you will deliver to them? How can you coordinate the activity of multiple teams if you don't have a plan?

The answer is that you need to change the way all of the parts of the business operate, and what you think of as a "plan." It's not enough to change the way you make your products and then leave the rest of the business to operate as if those changes weren't happening. The BBC tried to do this on its Digital Media Initiative project. That project needed to get non-software managers involved in the project as active participants rather than simply treat them as passive consumers. It needed the insight from those managers and other users in order to understand what users needed from the system. But, for whatever reason, managers declined to get involved in a meaningful way. In doing so, they starved the project of the oxygen it needed to survive—the feedback from the internal users—and contributed to the failure of the initiative. In order to create the kind of continuous conversation required to be successful in the digital world, we must understand that it will change the way people interact across the organization.

This means that we need to consider and change how our teams operate. We need to change how we conceive of, create, and market our products and services. We need to change the way we engage with our customers, stakeholders, and users during these processes.

These changes extend far beyond the work of software engineers and designers. The product managers have had to completely rethink the way they plan out their road maps and budgets. They have had to adjust their approach to coordination and planning.

Marketers and salespeople have had to adapt their approaches. They have had to change their sales models and their contracts with vendors. And of course, senior managers and executive leaders are faced with a tidal wave of bottom-up planning that challenges their expectations, their mandate, and their authority. In organizations that have been able to adjust their approaches to take advantage of this energy, we're seeing a smooth transition to the postindustrial age. But for organizations that continue to impose industrial-age centralized, top-down planning, we see a great deal of struggle. The gears, if you will, are grinding.

Adopting the Continuous Mindset: More Than Just Listening to the Customer

We're seeing many organizations that are in this gear-grinding state. Their technology teams are moving (perhaps tentatively) into the continuous rhythm and adopting the continuous mindset that makes it possible—but organizations are having trouble integrating these teams into the rest of the business. This is because the rest of the business doesn't yet have a model for moving to this new rhythm.

For years, companies have talked about the need to "listen to the customer." But listening alone is not enough. With digital technology beginning to power every element of business, we are going to see organizations facing the problem of managing uncertainty across many frontiers. Technology teams and theorists have converged on a way to handle this problem: use agile methods, frequent small experiments, deep collaboration between roles inside and outside businesses, and a continuous mindset. Sense and respond integrates these ideas and helps organizations listen and respond with great speed and flexibility. This goes beyond listening to customers. This is a continuous two-way conversation.

Sense and Respond Takeaways for Managers

✓ Because of the digital revolution, businesses face new levels of complexity and uncertainty.

✓ The industrial-age approach to managing uncertainty was to make detailed plans. Because software systems are complex, that approach does not work. Detailed plans break down in the face of reality.

✓ The best way to deal with uncertainty is to adopt a continuous, small-batch approach that is oriented toward learning your way forward.

✓ This approach, pioneered in the software world, is increasingly relevant across the business because many operations are tied in some way to software.

2

Sense and Respond

Continuous Learning

How does the sense and respond approach create two-way conversations with the market? How do teams use these conversations to create value? Let's consider an example.

In 2014, Time Inc. asked our company to help them build a new digital product offering for their *Cooking Light* magazine property. *Cooking Light* had spent the past thirty years building a reputation as a go-to source for healthy eating recipes. With the magazine industry in upheaval and paper-based subscriptions and ad revenue on the decline, the Cooking Light management team was faced with a challenge. It was sitting on an evergreen archive of healthy eating recipes, tips, and advice that traditionally had been delivered in one-way conversations—in other words, print. The need for the content was there, perhaps at an all-time high—Americans were moving away from fast food and toward healthy alternatives—and yet *Cooking Light* was failing to capitalize on this trend. Worse, its old business model was slowly failing. It needed to find new sources of revenue.

Prioritizing Learning over Delivery

The Cooking Light team needed to learn what kind of service would provide compelling value for readers. The team members had lots of ideas, but they didn't know which ones would work, so their first focus needed to be on learning and not on building anything.

This is the guiding principle for sense and respond organizations. Start by creating a conversation with your customers so that you can learn first, and refine and deliver second. Creating early, probing efforts will help determine which version of your idea resonates with your customers and will start the process of continuous learning. Without the learning, you risk delivering a product or service no one finds valuable. The sooner you discover whether your business strategies warrant further investment, the less time you waste on fruitless endeavors. In other words, the sooner you can find out whether you're wrong, the better.

The Cooking Light team members decided to test what they felt was their best idea—a new kind of diet service that periodically provided healthy recipes to users' email addresses: the Cooking Light Diet. They kicked off their learning efforts by creating a *landing page test*: a single-page website designed to market a new product or service, usually before the service actually exists. The team created three versions of this page. Each version contained variants of three elements:

- A clear description of the service

- The cost of the service

- A way for customers to sign up for a waiting list for the service

OK, there was a fourth element: it looked great, too.

These pages were the first version of the product. They didn't do much but were designed to start the conversation. If the test worked, it would help the team learn very quickly how to approach the customers it wanted to reach. If it didn't work, the team hadn't invested very much time or effort, and it could afford to try again.

The Cooking Light team members wanted to learn first—to sense—whether their ideas warranted further investment, and landing pages are low-risk learning tools. These kinds of early product iterations allow a team to sense customer interest, intent, perception of value, and price sensitivity. It is a fast way to learn. The effort to create and launch a landing page test, or even three, is trivial compared with building a fully functional service.

The amount of effort that went into this process was measured in days. A typical landing page takes a day or so to create, and you typically have useful results from the test within a week. Compared with traditional market research activities that normally take weeks or months, the team got a sense of the market very quickly.

In this first test, the team got great news: existing readers as well as nonreaders of *Cooking Light* were signing up for a waiting list for this new service at well-above-average rates. This high rate of engagement with the early product validated the team's desire to invest further and build the next version of the product.

Embracing Uncertainty: Questions Instead of Plans

The Cooking Light Diet team started with two things: a strategic objective and a list of questions. This is a remarkably modest and humble approach to a major new initiative. But facing all the unknowns—the uncertainty discussed in chapter 1—the team members felt they had little choice.

They saw it this way: between their current state (declining subscriptions and ad revenues) and their desired end state (a high-value service that would drive revenue growth by leveraging existing assets and strengths) there was a fog. They could see several steps into the fog (a desire for their content, a willingness to pay for it), but beyond that the path was obscured. What service should they build? How should they implement it? Which market segment should they focus on first?

The more typical, industrial-age approach would have been to create a detailed plan before the team began working. Indeed, this team had enough budget to take many steps in any single direction and hope it was headed in the right way. It could have spent a lot of money and time this way. However, the team members realized this approach was risky. Given that a fog hid all but the next few steps, the team risked going off a cliff. Every small step that gathered evidence—for example, the landing page test—allowed team members to sense new information, reduce uncertainty, and adjust their direction.

Landing page tests, experimentation, and continuous learning from the market are all elements of the lean startup methodology, an approach defined by Eric Ries in his popular book of the same name.[1] Ries proposed that we think of startups and other new, high-risk endeavors as experiments. The point of the experiment is not to determine whether an organization *can* build a new service or product. Instead, these experiments, predicated on collecting market feedback quickly, determine whether the organization *should* work on them at all. In other words, he's proposing that we consider market risk first, and technical risk second.

Lean startup is derived from Toyota's production system, also known as lean manufacturing. Taiichi Ohno, the father of lean thinking, worked with Eiji Toyoda at Toyota in postwar Japan to create a system to maximize value, make efficient use of limited capital, and eliminate waste. The two men believed that a system—a company, a product, a project—is always moving from a condition of doubt toward a condition of certainty in an ongoing quest for perfection. Each step in the direction of perfection and customer value is a valuable step. Everything else is waste.

Understanding the New Unit of Progress: Moving from Question to Question

Learning, moving from doubt to certainty, is often a process of trial and error. Trial and error is how we learn to walk, ride a bicycle, read, or play an instrument. In other words, we learn through action. When we put teams on projects, then, we want them to be able to act and, specifically, act in ways that bring learning.

In the older, industrial-age model, we tended to rely on careful advance study in order to learn. By the time we got to action, we assumed the learning was done. The sense and respond approach is different. We place less emphasis on up-front study and more emphasis on learning through action. We want to ensure our teams have the opportunity to try new things and that we don't fault them for their "failed" attempts. Each answer a team collects— positive or negative—is a unit of progress. It adds to team members' collective knowledge and allows them to ask a better question—in other words, to have a better conversation with the market—next time.

By now, the Cooking Light Diet team had answered its first set of questions. The landing page tests helped team members find an idea that had merit; it promised to move them toward their strategic goal, and they had built a substantial list of customers who were willing to pay for the service. The team was now ready to move to the next set of questions. It was time to figure out in more detail what content and features would be valuable to customers.

The team members knew they could spend weeks figuring out which features to build, how the system should work, and what it would look like. Instead, they again prioritized learning. They decided to launch a pilot version of the service. In this experiment they took the first twelve names on the waiting list and let them into the service. This was all very exciting for the participants, except for one thing: there was no service, at least not one that ran on software. Instead the team created what's called a *Wizard of Oz* test, so called because although the system appears to be operated by technology, in fact it's all powered by a man behind the curtain, just as in the movie.

The Cooking Light Diet team maintained a dialogue using email and phone interviews of the first cohort of participants in the new service. Members used the information they collected during these conversations to create menus for each participant by hand. They plugged the menus into a nicely designed email template and emailed them to each customer weekly. At the end of each week, members of the team held phone conversations with their new customers to understand which elements of the new service were valuable. They asked which recipes participants cooked. They asked what extra content was valuable. They asked about the shopping and planning process. They tried to understand what would make the service more compelling. The team built no web pages, wrote almost no code, and spent zero marketing dollars. And yet their customers experienced a new service. Through these person-to-person and low-tech interactions, the Cooking Light Diet team members continued the conversation they had started with the landing page tests. In doing so they were building a rhythm of learning loops that would sustain their progress throughout the project.

Wizard of Oz services are sometimes called *concierge services*, because they rely on a great deal of personal interaction between service provider and customer. This front-row seat to customer interaction and feedback creates a valuable two-way conversation between your organization and your customers and users. This conversation allows teams to focus their efforts on the features that deliver the highest customer value.

Next, the Cooking Light Diet team began to gradually transition the service—one piece at a time—to automation. To do this, members continued to run the service manually until they had clear evidence that automation was needed, and then they built only the smallest amount of software that would address the need. Sometimes, the evidence was qualitative; they would talk to a few customers and hear a pattern of feedback. At other times, especially as the service grew, the evidence was quantitative. They would see from system metrics that certain features weren't being used as often as they expected and would design a response. In this way, one feature at a time, the team deployed the service. With each new, slightly more sophisticated release of the service, team members would sense what the need was from the market and then respond with continuous updates.

Not only was the team able to continuously test its ideas and refine its thinking, but also the management team played a crucial role here by creating the context in which the team could work in this way. Specifically, the management team used the following tactics:

- *Allowed the team to make mistakes*—as long as they were relatively small and the team learned from them

- *Provided freedom, within clearly stated constraints, to make their own decisions*—so time wasn't wasted waiting for executive feedback

- *Placed value on customer behavior as a measure of progress*—and not on the number of features the team was shipping

This is a good example of the mechanics used by sensing organizations. Companies that value learning provide teams with business problems to solve, clear constraints within which they can operate, and clear success metrics. The teams then figure out how best to solve these problems, moving from question to question, with the success criteria serving as the barometer of progress.

Defining Vision and Success

One common question about working this way revolves around vision and strategy. It's easy to see a team operating this way and mistakenly conclude that because team members are not certain what comes next, they don't have a plan or a vision. Or worse, they are simply optimizing their service based on data, with no unifying thesis driving their work.

This is not the point of sense and respond. Instead, sense and respond is a way of *pursuing* a vision, using evidence collected through a continuous, two-way conversation with the market to make decisions. This approach uses alignment with goals (rather than a detailed plan) to coordinate the activities of teams. In fact, the stronger the vision, the easier it is to use sense and respond methods.

The Cooking Light Diet team is only one small-scale example of how this works. Starting with a simple idea—to "create a healthy diet service for people who love our recipes in order to produce revenue for our brand"—the team was able to follow that vision to create a successful service.

Value Is Defined by Users, Customers, and the Market

If you look at the team's statement, it's weighted toward what the service will do for the business. What value will it create for customers, though? The Cooking Light Diet team knew that, in order to be successful, team members would need to understand what customers found valuable and orient their work toward delivering it. As the team members moved forward and learned more, they adopted a second vision statement, one that expressed the problem from the customer's point of view: "I need easy, delicious meals that I know will give me the results I need to improve my health."

These statements became the team's two benchmarks. Would the features it was working on solve the problems customers faced in trying to achieve this outcome? Could the team do it in a way that provided value to the business?

The New Definition of "Done"

In the industrial-age mindset, *success* was the launch of a product—especially if the launch was on time and on budget—because, in the industrial age, the connection between a product and its use were usually pretty clear. A quarter-inch drill produces a quarter-inch hole. In traditional and well-understood product categories, you could be reasonably certain that if you could make something that worked, met demand, and was priced correctly, you would be successful.

But as our products have gotten more complex and as customers' expectations have risen, our level of uncertainty about our services has also grown. Simply making a thing is no longer good enough, because the link between purpose and actual use is less clear. What is the "use" for Facebook? How will people use the videos they shoot on their smartphones? If you put a diet service on people's phones, how will they use it? In the information age, we have so many new situations that it's hard to rely on a traditional understanding of the market. How do we know what to make? How can we know what people will do with it? In the information age, the best way to understand value is to let our customers tell us what they value. In other words, value is not what we say it is: it's what our customers say it is.

So making a thing, creating an *output* of some sort, is not our goal. Instead, success is the extent to which we achieve an *outcome* and help our customers achieve an outcome they seek. Make it easier to connect to family and friends, make it easier to find healthy food in a supermarket—these are outcomes that create value for the customer and, if delivered correctly, to the business in turn. This is the new definition of a product or service that is "done." And it's an evolving target. In a world of continuous learning and real-time response, we can always continue to improve. We move from initiative to initiative based on our perception of how much positive change further investment will make. Although we continue to use it, the word *done* doesn't really make sense any more, given software's continuous nature. In sense and respond organizations, "done" simply means we've maximized the experience or have decided to shift our priorities to other outcomes.

Learning from a Cautionary Tale: Building without Sensing

Amazon's 2014 Fire Phone disaster is a classic counterexample and, oddly, one that comes from the very same company that developed and frequently uses many of the sense and respond techniques we're discussing—a company we laud in chapter 1 for that reason.

Motivated by consumers' increasing use of mobile devices, Amazon began the Fire Phone effort in 2010, just as the iPhone 4 was hitting the market. Mobile users were becoming a more important source of traffic to Amazon, and the company wanted more control of the mobile store than Apple would allow. Apple's rules about what companies can and can't do in iOS apps include strict rules about commerce, including one that stipulates that Apple gets a 30 percent share of each in-app sale.[2] (The reason you can't buy a book on the iOS Kindle app is that Amazon doesn't want to pay Apple 30 percent of each sale.) So Amazon created the Fire Phone initiative to solve a business problem: it wanted complete control over the store that its customers visited on their mobile devices.

But what would be the value to customers? They struggled to find it, in part because of a strict culture of secrecy around this product. Jeff Bezos, CEO of Amazon, had lots of ideas for cool features. But cool and valuable are not the same thing. Over time, Bezos exerted an increasingly heavier hand in the design and development of the Fire Phone and, according to published reports, ignored feedback from his team that questioned his approach.[3] There was no conversation with the market here, only Bezos talking. He insisted that the phone have a series of flashy features like Dynamic Perspective, a 3-D display that didn't require special glasses and could be seen from all angles; but it delivered little consumer value. Bezos assumed that flashy hardware features would make the phone more desirable to consumers than an iPhone. Without a continuous two-way conversation with his target audience to guide the development of these features, though, Bezos was making a huge guess.

He guessed wrong. Four years later, in July 2014, the Fire Phone went on sale in the United States. Within days it was clear that consumers were unimpressed—with the design, with the ecosystem, and with the gimmicky features Bezos had pushed for so hard. Priced at $199, the Fire Phone was intended to compete directly with Apple's iPhone, but consumers didn't see the value. Instead, they saw it for what it was—a way to easily get to Amazon's store in a way that was better for Amazon but not significantly better for customers.

After a $170 million write-down of unsold inventory, the Fire Phone was available for 99 cents before finally being sunset in late 2015. The behind-the-scenes stories reveal the arrogance in the top-down decision-making process that Bezos led.[4] Although people on the team pushed back, they ended up deferring to the boss. After all, he'd been right many times before. Why wouldn't he be right again this time?

It might have helped if Bezos had listened to the market. Had he approached some of these decisions as assumptions to be tested and questions to be answered, rather than hunches to be followed blindly, things might have been different.

Making Perfect Plans Versus Making Plans to Learn

The top-down, change-resistant planning we see in the Fire Phone story is all too common. It's the norm in large organizations. Most often it's expressed in a document called a *feature road map*. This is a compelling document. It gives a clear sense of where we are, where we're headed, and what features we'll build to get from here to there. It provides a sense of progress and serves as a motivational tool for teams, managers, executives, and, often, external partners and stakeholders. It sets expectations about when features will be done.

It's also a complete fabrication.

Imagine, for a second, the product manager for the Cooking Light Diet team committing to a feature road map at the beginning of the initiative. She would commit to a specific feature set, pricing strategy, and delivery dates. Then after each experiment and set of customer conversations, she would have to revise the road map and go back to her stakeholders to get it approved, each time watching as her credibility eroded. While this is happening, the team members would be waiting for approval, their productivity slowing to a crawl. Their learning would be causing problems.

The alternative to feature road maps is to make looser plans and then adjust them as you learn. (We talk about this in more detail in chapter 5.) The Cooking Light Diet team kept a few lists that it used to drive the project. The first was a list of questions, assumptions, and risks. As team members learned, they moved through this list, answering questions, paying down risk, and adding new questions. The second list was a list of *possible* features. These were features that the team and stakeholders thought they might need but for which they had no evidence of actual need. Each week, the team reviewed the feedback it received from talking to users and from reviewing system metrics. It cross-referenced that feedback with the possible-features list and then selected its priorities for the coming week.

Testing Assumptions

Business school graduates, certified project managers, and product owners are taught that their teams need requirements in order to execute effectively. So teams make detailed plans—they *elaborate the requirements*, in the language of the trade—and then estimate the amount of work it will take to complete the plan. They report this to managers, who then bake all this into financial models, resource allocations, and funding plans. These, in turn, are shared with executive leadership and, if the company is publicly traded, the stock markets. After all this public and detailed commitment, everyone is ready to move forward with *the plan*.

Sound familiar? It should. It's how most companies plan their fiscal years, program-level funding decisions, and project deadlines.

It's surprising that we keep doing it, though, because this kind of plan *is always wrong.*

Why? It's because these plans are based on assumptions. On guesses.

If we're lucky, we'll be working with educated guesses based on domain expertise, years of industry and corporate performance data, deep knowledge of the customer, and a finger on the pulse of competitive companies. At worst, as with the Amazon Fire Phone, the guesses are only one person's opinions (often the highest-paid person). Although this approach may work in industries with long histories and very low levels of uncertainty, the ubiquitous use of software has increased the pace of change for customer expectations, lowered the barriers to entry for new competitors, and made domainwide disruption a reality for every industry. Working in this new reality, with these new levels of uncertainty, makes assumption-driven planning incredibly risky.

Forming Hypotheses

Every project begins with assumptions. There's no getting around this fact. We assume we know our customers (and whom our future customers will be). We assume we know what the competition is doing and where our industry is headed. We assume we can predict the stability of our markets. These assumptions are predicated on our ability to predict the future. But the last time we checked, this was still not a core feature of humans.

So if we accept that we're always starting with assumptions, the real question becomes, What do we do about the risk of being wrong? The first step is to identify our assumptions. How much of what we think we know is fact, and how much of it is just the stuff we assume is true?

So declaring assumptions is the first step in figuring out what we know for sure and what we need to sense. The next question is then, How can we learn what we need to learn? Advocates of lean startup recommend using the scientific method to test our assumptions. This means expressing our assumptions as testable hypotheses and then running a series of experiments to find the truth.

Let's take the Fire Phone as an example. If you were to declare a series of assumptions about the project and express them as a hypothesis, it might look like this:

> We believe we can achieve an increase in mobile customer acquisition and sales if our customers choose to access our products and services with a dedicated Amazon-branded mobile phone instead of with their iPhone and other iOS devices.

Looking at this proposition this way, we can start to identify risks in our thinking. We're assuming that we'll make more money if customers have an Amazon phone instead of an iPhone. This seems like a pretty safe assumption, perhaps even a statement of fact: we won't have to pay Apple a cut of any purchase made on a Fire Phone. But the next part is more troubling. It assumes customers would switch to Amazon Fire Phones but doesn't say why. So we need another hypothesis.

> We believe that customers will switch from iPhones to Fire Phones because they value our Dynamic Perspective 3-D display.

Looked at in so many words, the risk seems obvious.

Hypotheses serve as a mirror of our thinking. They position our assumptions in a way that makes us question our original thoughts.

Usually, we want to start with the biggest questions and work our way down into the details. Typically, you would start with questions like these:

- Does the business problem exist?

- Does the customer need exist?

- How do we know whether this feature or service will address that need?

As you sit down with your teams to plan out your next initiatives, ask them these questions.

- What's the most important thing or things we need to learn first?

- What's the fastest, most efficient way to learn that?

Once you answer those questions, you can move to the next set of questions and invest accordingly.

Sensing, Using Big Data, and Reducing Risk

The *Cooking Light* story shows how a single small team can create something new using a sense and respond approach. But what about a big company working on existing businesses?

Canadian Tire is a C$13 billion, hundred-year-old conglomerate of hardware stores, sporting goods stores, and stores that sell automotive products—and a Canadian icon. It's also a pioneer of *big data*, using the data it collects on customer behavior and purchases to continuously improve its business.

For years, Canadian Tire operated a loyalty program called Canadian Tire "Money." The paper-based "currency" had been in use since 1961 and was a beloved staple of Canadian culture. It had even been used as bartering currency in times past. With more than fifty years' worth of historical and cultural inertia hanging over any changes to this system, Canadian Tire recognized that digitizing Canadian Tire "Money" would risk losing loyal customers and damaging the brand; but the company also knew it had an opportunity to learn more about customer behavior if it could move the program into a digital form. So, in the past few years, it began to plan a transition.[5] For the company, there was a clear benefit to going digital. For its customers, though, the benefit was less obvious.

The company's hypothesis was that through a gentle transition to its mobile app and debit cards, it could sway the population away from the paper version and find ways to create value for customers. To limit the risk of a faulty launch, Canadian Tire launched the app-based version of Canadian Tire "Money" in its Nova Scotia store only. As customers slowly switched over to the digital version, Canadian Tire monitored the transition both by watching the numbers and by talking to customers. It turns out that people began switching quite easily to the new format. Many of them already had the Canadian Tire mobile app on their phones (of which "Money" was now a part) and were accustomed to digital payments.

Sometimes, the things we assume will be big problems turn out to be trivial. What we value inside a company—in this case, the traditional, paper-based version of Canadian Tire "Money"—may be understood differently outside our walls. Still, by limiting the launch to a single location, the company was able to take on a comfortable level of risk as compared with a broader national launch.

The move to digital was worth it, because it helped create a new conversation with customers about what they were buying and what Canadian Tire could do to improve the business for customers.

As customers began using the digital version, new data flowed in at scale. By monitoring this data, the company began to see consumer patterns emerging. It noticed, for example, distinct opportunities to improve the way seasonal products were organized in the Nova Scotia store. This new sensing ability revealed that customers were struggling to find all the products necessary to complete their seasonal lawn care work. Products were organized in the store by product type (lawn mowers with power tools, for example) rather than by related function—"lawn care," for example. This forced customers to walk up and down several aisles to find everything they needed, and they often failed to do so.

In response, Canadian Tire reorganized the stores around specific tasks to make it easier for customers to find everything they needed in one aisle. Then, again, it watched the data, and the data showed that the new plan worked. It improved customer experience in the stores, and it resulted in a sales increase in the Nova Scotia store.

Since the successful test in Nova Scotia, Canadian Tire has continued to roll out the digital currency more broadly. It's important to note that in this case, the sensing capability is digital, but the responses are made with traditional in-store retail tactics. Sense and respond isn't limited to the digital domain; it's just enabled by it.

Understanding That Sense and Respond Is Culture, Too

So far, we've talked about sense and respond in terms of process. But it also has a cultural dimension.

Recall our discussion about uncertainty. Sense and respond is effective in the face of uncertainty because it actively embraces the idea. It starts with the notions that we don't have all the information we'd like to have, and we're not sure whether our plans will be effective. In other words, it starts with a certain amount of humility, a quality that is often in short supply in business.

The team structure on the Cooking Light Diet project is worth considering. It was a small team, consisting of a few designers, a few software developers, a product manager, an editor, a nutritionist, and a few other specialists who stepped in from time to time. These folks worked together on a daily basis, making and adjusting plans, interpreting data, working with customers, and making decisions about the direction of the service. The work flow was deeply collaborative, and the conversations were structured so that the different points of view on the team were understood to be an advantage. This team setup let the team move quickly and bring diverse expertise to bear on problems.

On a team like this, there's no place for cowboys, ninjas, rock stars, or gurus. (The Lone Ranger wasn't much of a collaborator.) Folks who are invested in their own ideas will have a hard time working with a team that wants to listen to the market, gather evidence, and find the best idea, regardless of its source. Those personalities don't work on a sensing team.

Including Executives

The team mentality must start at the executive level. Leaders must set and communicate direction and then allow the team to gather information, learn, and react. We witnessed the benefits of this type of leadership firsthand with the executives sponsoring the Cooking Light Diet project. They recognized the business problem, assigned a team to solve it, gave the team measurable success targets in terms of revenue and strategic fit, defined the constraints of its autonomy, and then got out of its way. In return, the team worked continuously with the leaders to keep them up to date on what it was learning. Team members presented evidence about which ideas were working, where more investment was (or wasn't) merited, where their plans were progressing, and where expectations needed to be adjusted. And leadership responded. This continuous cycle of communication gave the Cooking Light Diet team the freedom to explore its way to the best possible solution.

Over the course of eighteen months the diet service grew from a manual service that served twelve customers to a fully automated healthy-eating service with an annual run rate of $1 million and growing. The features the team built in to this service were never predetermined in a requirements document or prescribed by the executives. Instead, the service started with a vision and was built by a team that continuously sensed what the market wanted and responded by delivering only features that created value.

Pixar CEO Ed Catmull summarizes this approach beautifully in his book *Creativity, Inc.*

> I believe the best managers acknowledge and make room for what they do not know—not just because humility is a virtue but because until one adopts that mindset, the most striking breakthroughs cannot occur. I believe that managers must loosen the controls, not tighten them. They must accept risk; they must trust the people they work with and strive to clear the path for them; and always, they must pay attention to and engage with anything that creates fear. Moreover, successful leaders embrace the reality that their models may be wrong or incomplete. Only when we admit what we don't know can we ever hope to learn it.[6]

We talk more about culture and team structure in Part II, but it's important to recognize here that working this way is a change—in some cases, an enormous change—from the way things are currently done in most large companies.

Putting It All Together

What does it look like when you put it all together? Here's an example of the sense and respond cycle in which a company called Forward 3D used this approach to create a new business.[7]

Forward 3D is a search marketing company; it runs advertising campaigns on search engines based on specific keywords users type in. This means that it needs to collect and analyze data on the things people search for on the internet. Executives thought they might be able to use this data to help clients do more than run marketing campaigns. They thought they could help clients find new business opportunities.

The team decided to run an experiment first. Within the search data it collected, it discovered that many people searched for pet supplies, but there were not a lot of businesses advertising against these searches. When team members dug a little deeper, they discovered that searches for parrot cages seemed particularly popular, and there were few businesses serving this need.

They decided to probe this insight further. Using basic services available to any entrepreneur on the web, they set up a test page for selling parrot cages online. This was a landing page test, very similar to the tactic used by the Cooking Light Diet team. The Forward 3D page didn't actually allow people to buy any cages; it just let people express interest, a two-way conversation. And the interest was clear.

Based on these results, the team started actually selling parrot cages through the JustCages.com domain it had set up for this purpose.

The team set up the barest of operations. It used drop shippers to fulfill orders, so the company never had to take the financial risk of holding any inventory. This proved profitable very quickly, and the team responded again by improving the sophistication of the website. Ultimately, as it gained confidence in the business, it took more of the operations (and risk) in-house, including stocking inventory in a warehouse.

As general manager Martin McNulty said, "What we absolutely didn't do was build a beautiful website on day one. What we really did was figure out the demand side first."[8] In other words, the team worked out the riskiest assumption first—that there really was demand for the service—before moving on to learn what it would take to actually operate the business. Team members tested each step along the way with the smallest, lowest-investment solutions available. In other words, they set up a continuous sense and respond loop with the target audience. And each time they learned something, Forward 3D responded quickly to capitalize on the opportunity. Today they are one of the largest sellers of pet cages online.

Sense and Respond Takeaways for Managers

✓ Sense and respond in practice is about small, autonomous teams experimenting and learning in pursuit of a vision or a strategy.

✓ Teams learn their way forward by making loose plans, running small experiments, and testing their assumptions as they move forward.

✓ Teams focus on continuously uncovering value through a two-way conversation between company and market.

✓ Value is defined in customer-centered terms.

✓ This approach can work for startup teams and within large companies.

✓ Teams use any data they can find, both qualitative and quantitative.

✓ The approach works best with small, cross-functional teams.

✓ Sense and respond is more than a process; it's a culture. It requires humility on the part of team members and leadership.

3

Why Companies Resist

Overcoming Obstacles
and Objections

When we wrote our first book, *Lean UX*, our goal was to show modern practitioners—the designers, developers, product managers, and other staffers who form digital teams—an effective way to work with digital technology. The approach laid out in that book has proven popular with the hands-on people working in digital technology. But the method is not without its critics, and it's not without obstacles.

The most significant feedback we heard about *Lean UX* comes down to this: "We love this approach, but we can't do it here." As we dug deeper into the reasons, it became clear why this challenge was most prominent: most companies are not set up to take advantage of technology-driven continuous learning. Indeed, in 2015, a *Harvard Business Review* study on digital leadership revealed that many managers are aware of the challenges posed by digital technology: the risk that it will disrupt their business and the need to create an effective response.[1] Many of these leaders even have a clear picture of how they need to proceed. And yet the overwhelming majority of these managers face challenges in turning their organizations around. The "way we've always done it"—annual financial budgets, long-term strategic planning, discipline-based silos, incentive structures based on production quotas—proves to be too hard to overcome.

But it's not impossible. Organizations are solving these problems and making these changes. Here, then, are some of the major obstacles to working effectively to build organizations that learn continuously, along with examples of companies overcoming these obstacles.

Overcoming the Steve Jobs Myth

If you talk about uncertainty, humility, and market feedback long enough, you're sure to crash headfirst into the legend of Steve Jobs. People hold up Apple in general, and Steve Jobs in particular, as a model of a certain kind of deliberate process, one in which visionary leadership and force of will, combined with detail-oriented planning and an obsessive pursuit of perfection, are able to dictate taste in the marketplace. "Where is the experimentation?" people ask. "Where is the humility?"

To some extent one has to acknowledge a certain level of genius in Steve Jobs. Also worth noting is that very few leaders possess those same qualities—despite their proclamations to the contrary. And yet, for those who believe they possess a Steve Jobs-like amount of insight, little will dissuade them.

A deeper look reveals a more complex story behind the Steve Jobs genius myth. It's true that Apple has created some of the most successful consumer products ever. However, its successes are, for the most part, ones in which one person interacts with one machine to do one thing. Apple's failures in software (remember MobileMe?) and social networking (Ping) demonstrate that the development process that serves the company well in some spheres is not sufficient to deal with most complex software-based services. iTunes, formerly a model of simplicity and power, is now routinely held up as an example of corporate bloatware.

Apple's traditional process, however, is filled with experimentation; it just experiments in secret. Rumors that Apple was working on a phone circulated for years before the first iPhone shipped. The design press is filled with photos of early Apple prototypes. Prototypes, as powerful as they are, can teach you only so much. They can't reveal what happens when thousands of people are using your software at the same time; they can't help you discover and capture the value presented by emergent behavior. As with the Amazon Fire Phone, covert efforts can reveal only so much. At some point, the ideas have to be tested in the wild.

What Apple can teach us, though, is the power of vision and the ability of vision and culture to create alignment. A manager who worked at an Apple partner company in the 1990s told us a story of working with an Apple team to create a product bundle. Apple had sought out this partner because Apple wanted to include one of the company's products in the bundle. But first, the Apple managers wanted changes to the partner product. Specifically, they objected to the setup process the product required. "It has to work out of the box," an Apple manager said, expressing the cultural value Apple places on customer experience. "If it doesn't work out of the box," he said, "we don't ship it."

This is the power of alignment. It's a cultural value that everyone in the firm knows and that guides decision making. This obsession—with quality, with design, with out-of-the-box experience—wasn't something only Steve Jobs delivered. It was something he was able to make the entire firm deliver.

Being Paid to Ship Product, Not to Learn

Perhaps the most challenging and difficult objection to overcome is your company's reward and compensation structure. At the end of the day, your staff and, most important, your middle managers will do what they get paid to do. If your company's bonus and promotion structure rewards on-time, on-budget delivery, the teams will optimize for delivery. If your salespeople promise features and bake those promises into contracts, your teams will have little opportunity to change course in the face of learning.

This is the industrial-age factory model applied to modern, technology-driven products: rewarding people for making things rather than rewarding them for making the right things. It functions based on the continued belief that digitally powered products and services can and should be stamped out like parts on an assembly line. The faster and cheaper we can do that, the more we'll succeed. This belief manifests as managers explicitly telling staff what to do. It's still the dominant model in most companies.

It turns out, though, that, if teams' goals are set in terms of changing customer behavior rather than shipping a set of features, they end up delivering superior results. Adopting this model requires that middle managers take a leap of faith that it will help them achieve their goals faster than the traditional ways they've used to date.

Notably, incentives are not something that teams themselves can change. This is a responsibility that falls squarely on upper management's shoulders. As you consider how to plan your next set of initiatives, ask yourself the following questions:

- If we ship a new set of features on time and on budget, how will we know they were the right features?

- Can we measure the success of these new initiatives in terms of business and customer outcomes?

- How can I empower my teams to make better use of the continuous stream of information they receive from the market every day to build two-way conversations?

- How can I reward them for using that information to choose which work to do and which work not to do?

We explore this more deeply in chapter 5, when we explore outcome-based planning.

Complying with Regulations and Legal Requirements

The idea of continuous market feedback and continuous change can seem like a mirage if you're working in an industry with strict regulatory oversight. These organizations are often constrained by the need to follow well-defined procedures to stay within the law, including regulatory review and approval, before releasing products and services to the public. Technology may speed up our collection and synthesis of data, but it can't speed up bureaucracy.

However, we can change our attitudes toward compliance. One chief risk officer we worked with in the financial services industry recognized that his staff was functioning as a series of "red lights" to impede the progress of product teams. His goal, in the face of continuous two-way conversations and ever-increasing competitive threats, was to figure out how to redistribute his people among the product teams so that they functioned as a series of "green lights" as they moved toward production—turning red only when an important issue arose.

Private sector companies can handle this obstacle in a variety of ways. Many companies create small innovation and discovery teams to explore new ideas in a safe way. They test ideas on a small scale and within safe limits using what we call a *sandbox*, a tactic we explain in chapter 7. Additionally, large companies frequently work with regulators and legislators to explain their intentions and clear the way for the work they want to do. In 2015, for example, the Taxi and Limousine Commission in New York proposed rules that would require Uber, Lyft, and other ride-hailing services to submit their apps for approval whenever they made changes to the user interface. Leaders from these firms, and from the tech industry at large, met with regulators to explain how modern software teams operate and why these regulations would be onerous. Regulators withdrew the proposal.[2]

Public sector organizations also face these challenges frequently, but, again, working with regulators to interpret rules and clarify boundaries can help. One manager at a US government agency told us of ongoing efforts to clarify rules about what are called *Privacy Impact Assessments*, a risk-assessment process that can often stand in the way of rapid iteration. As teams increasingly adopt sense and respond methods, we expect to see their work driving changes in the way regulatory oversight works as well.

Adopting Rapid Change in Safety-Critical Work

There are contexts in which safety concerns would keep us from releasing frequent live experiments to learn from the market. For example, you wouldn't want to A/B test the software controls of a jumbo jet. And this leads to the somewhat unsurprising observation that these methods do not always apply in every context. There are many mature industries that develop safety-critical systems and have mature practices that allow controlled tests under safe conditions. These industries typically have a strong engineering culture and tradition and are building systems with high levels of predictability. That said, it would be a mistake to think that sense and respond can't be used in these industries in the right context. We predict an increase in the use of sense and respond techniques used alongside traditional techniques in even the most traditional and safety-conscious industries.

Airbus Group, for example, has begun experimenting with innovation labs that can develop and test ideas quickly.[3] As an example, one project coming out of the inaugural lab in Toulouse, France, is an innovative way to ensure the security of a parked airplane. Currently this requires a labor-intensive effort that must be followed without fail each time an airplane is taken out of service for maintenance or extended time on the ground. Teams working in the lab are figuring out ways to automate this process through a series of sensors located on sensitive areas of the planes; the sensors are monitored in real time by airport staff. By compartmentalizing the learning effort, Airbus is minimizing the risk to its ongoing operations. These labs reduce the amount of investment each idea gets, allowing them to operate in parallel with the broader business without disruption or safety risks. Once an idea has proven its merit, Airbus can take the next steps to productize it or integrate it into the broader manufacturing process.

And General Electric has begun a program called Digital Twins that involves creating digital simulations of hardware products. A jet engine might have a "virtual twin" specific to the engine running entirely in software. This allows GE to monitor real-time performance of that specific engine and also to experiment with new engine features and settings in the digital realm without having to take safety risks in the real world.

Using This Method in Large Companies

It can be difficult to carve out permission to work this way in large companies. Often, this is simply because any change is hard in large companies.

Usually, a single team with few dependencies and an enlightened manager can simply start adopting some of these practices, and, over time, its success will validate its methods. But as these practices are scaled up to multiteam programs, the dependencies, communication, and coordination challenges can be daunting.

Entrepreneur coach and adviser David J. Bland took on these challenges on a small scale with a team at Toyota in 2014. Bland engaged with the legendary carmaker to help it test new in-car features that were not quite ready for production. In one project, Toyota wanted to see whether redesigning its vehicles to better integrate with gas pumps would improve the convenience of refueling for customers.

Normally, Toyota would build a team for this initiative and plan out its budget for the next twelve months. The financing for the endeavor would come from business plans that would predict not only the necessary level of funding but also the ROI that would come from that investment in various future time frames.

Bland and his team challenged this traditional model by starting with a limited budget and focusing on building rough prototypes of the proposed service. These prototypes were hacked together with basic web-based software and some automobile dashboard components Toyota made available. The team then recruited users from Craigslist and Facebook. Team members showed them their ideas, had them try to use them, and learned quickly which parts held consumer value and, equally important, which ones didn't. Based on the insights driven by these two-way conversations (in this case, face-to-face, not digital), Toyota was able to make an evidence-based decision on further investment in this project.

This small team was allowed to operate independently, something that gave it the freedom to build in the sense and respond cycles it needed before deciding on next steps. Its isolation from the day-to-day bureaucracy of the broader organization gave team members the freedom to move at their own pace, learn about their ideas, and adjust course as they learned.

But more often than not, in large companies, teams *do* have dependencies; frequently, there are teams waiting on other teams, waiting for a specific piece of work to be completed. In these cases, any change in the working plan needs to be coordinated. The lone wolf approach won't work here.

It is possible to coordinate the work of multiple teams using sense and respond methods. At Westpac, the largest bank in Australia, for example, teams create a simple outcome-based charter to align the activities of multiple teams in large programs. They use vision statements that are carefully crafted so as to guide execution across multiple teams but still allow individual teams the freedom to experiment and learn. In chapter 5, we go into more detail about how Westpac and other large organizations do this.

Overcoming Government Obstacles

We've made the case that working this way requires self-directed teams with freedom of action and permission to fail. Nowhere are these qualities harder to find than in government. The layers of obstacles are myriad: laws, regulations, and procedures; politics, elections, and budgets; twenty-four-hour news cycles and public accountability. It's a wonder anything gets done. And yet the mission is to serve the people—perhaps the most customer-centered mission you can have. So can you unlock the potential of sense and respond to build a real-time two-way conversation in government?

We're starting to see the emergence of new government offices designed specifically to address this challenge, and, significantly, these organizations are fully committed to using sense and respond approaches. In the United Kingdom, the recently chartered Government Digital Service (GDS) describes its approach this way: "We always start with user needs. We are agile. We work to a set of Design Principles that guide us in everything we do. We believe in working openly, because making things open makes them better."[4] GDS is a leader in this movement, and it has been the model for similar organizations in the United States (18F and US Digital Service), Australia (The Digital Transformation Office), and elsewhere.

Working with Procurement Rules

One of the major challenges faced in government is procurement. Traditional rules require contracts with vendors that specify very precisely the features and functions of systems to be developed. As you've seen, though, this approach, designed to create accountability and ensure wise spending of taxpayer money, fails frequently and often quite spectacularly. But officials working in government frequently have no choice: Noah Kunin, infrastructure director at 18F, the US government's internal digital services agency, laid out the facts in three tweets in 2014.

> In order to create a web site in the Fed Gov that does *anything*, you need to read over 1,000 pages of mandatory policy.
>
> @noahkunin, 12 Dec 2014

If you have to spend money to build that web site, add another 2,000 pages to read. Want to store data? Another 200.

@noahkunin, 12 Dec 2014

If you follow that through and read some implementation guides, you're probably now at around 3,500 pages. This is a bureaucracy in crisis.

@noahkunin, 12 Dec 2014[5]

We've experienced this firsthand. A potential government client from the United States approached our company for help in developing a new system. The client imagined a powerful communication platform to connect state government and constituents—a modern two-way conversation system. It was an exciting and unique opportunity; nothing like it existed at the time. Needless to say, we wanted the project.

Project leads explained their goals to us: they wanted to reduce the millions of dollars spent annually on postage by replacing mailings with an electronic system. And they'd come prepared with a lengthy list of features they required by a specific date that they assumed would achieve this goal. But it became clear as we spoke that these assumptions were untested. Working with the project leads, we proposed a different approach, one designed to test assumptions and measure success in terms of reduction in postage costs—an outcome—rather than in terms of features built.

It didn't fly: our clients were forced to decline. They just couldn't sign a contract that didn't have a commitment to a specific set of features. Given the high cost of the project, budget approval would have to come from the state's attorney general, an elected position. It was an election year, and the attorney general was taking no chances.

The attorney general couldn't risk facing questions about authorizing the use of taxpayer money without a clear commitment from the vendor to build a system exactly as specified.

There is a movement to change all this. One of the first projects that the United Kingdom's GDS worked on was a new way of chartering projects—in other words, a new way to authorize spending. Recognizing that it was important to test assumptions (rather than define requirements) before funding system development, GDS spent eight months getting approval for a new chartering process that involves a discovery phase followed by an alpha phase. GDS describes it this way: "When designing a service it's impossible to predict everything upfront. Each project features many challenges, and in [the alpha phase] you will start exploring solutions for these."[6]

In the United States, 18F is also working on procurement rules. Since late 2015, it has been experimenting with new methods for engaging contractors and vendors and has been publishing the results of these experiments on its blog. By 2016, it had launched a pilot of this new approach and had signed on two government agencies to participate: the FBI and the US Department of the Treasury.[7] We are in the early days of this effort, but clearly the recognition is there, and the work to change the system has begun.

Lacking the Right People

It takes a certain kind of attitude to embrace a sense and respond style of work. People who thrive in this environment are curious and humble and comfortable with uncertainty. They're oriented toward learning and tend to be good at collaboration. They want feedback on their work, and they want to fix it if it's not right. Not everyone fits this description.

One of our clients, a women's fashion retailer, was working with us to build a more evidence-based approach to its digital product development process. Over the course of a couple of days' training, the teams were absorbing the sense and respond material and making progress. But when it came time to venture out into the field to interview customers, a small mutiny unfolded. Fifteen back-end engineers, folks who typically work as far away from the actual customer as one can get, had threatened to quit their jobs if they had to leave the office to speak with customers.

You can imagine our surprise at this turn of events. Here we were at the beginning of this client's training effort, and we were facing the possibility that this transformation might unravel before it even began. We pulled the client aside and used this incident as a teaching moment.

As it turned out, we were able to broker a compromise in which the engineers would still go out into the field but would function as notetakers. They wouldn't have to actually speak with any customers.

This was a learning moment for all of us. Creating two-way conversations with a sense and respond approach builds in feedback loops that aren't there now. This can be uncomfortable for members of your team. If you commit to this way of working, parting ways with some of your colleagues should be expected. Coming to terms with that will help your organization establish the right environment more quickly. And the sooner it's set up, the more it will attract like-minded individuals.

Successful sense and respond companies find people who *want* to work this way. You'll want to hire explorers, researchers, and problem solvers who are not content with the status quo. These folks are attracted to environments that already practice this way of working, which can be a catch-22. You can't hire the right people without the right environment, and you can't create the right environment without the right people. The good news is that there are likely people on your staff now who would prefer this way of working but who haven't yet had the chance. Find them, and give them the challenge they seek.

Protecting Your Brand as You Experiment

Brands make a promise. If you've been in business for a while, your customers have come to expect things from you. Quality. Service. Trustworthiness. You are understandably cautious about trying things without considering how your customers will feel about them. You don't want to risk alienating them or appear to be cluelessly trying things—stabbing at ideas in the dark.

These are all legitimate concerns. Some of the largest companies we've worked with have shared them. To work around them, many companies will run their experiments off-brand. They might launch new ideas under made-up company names, for example, or try things on such a small scale that it limits how much impact a bad test would have on the brand.

But some companies are willing to experiment in public. Nordstrom, a high-end US department store chain famous for customer service, made a video of one of its innovation teams experimenting in the store. The experiment—and the video, which has been widely viewed on YouTube—makes the brand look terrific: bold, fearless, and respectful and solicitous of customers' needs. Nordstrom is, in the words of strategist Christina Wodtke, "experimenting *with* their customers, not on their customers."[8]

Fearing It's a Fad

Design thinking, lean, Six Sigma, customer-driven innovation, lean startup, agile, OODA loops. Sound familiar? At one point or another, these ideas have all been the flavor of the month in management circles. And there's no doubt that ideas become trendy, gain favor, and seem as though they will save our companies, only to be discarded when, somehow, they don't live up to the hype. Perhaps you see the phrase *sense and respond* and think it's just another one to add to that list.

But what we're talking about is a response that has emerged to manage a newly present reality. Uncertainty, thanks to the nature of digital products and services, is here to stay, and we're going to need a way to move forward productively. Sense and respond is simply the label we've applied to a group of related approaches that seem to be our best way forward at the moment. These approaches embody the ideas of collaboration, continuous learning, and evidence-based decision making. They're about gathering evidence and paying down risk in an ongoing way.

These approaches include process, but sense and respond is not only a process. They include culture change, but sense and respond is not simply an attitude. Sense and respond is the most recent version of an approach to managing uncertainty that has been with us for a long time. It certainly predates the Industrial Revolution. So even though fads may come and go, technology is here to stay. Sense and respond is how you manage in the digital world.

Sense and Respond Takeaways for Managers

✓ Although no single approach is right for every context, sense and respond approaches can be and are being used in places that might seem unlikely at first blush.

✓ Sense and respond is not an abdication of a vision; it is often the best way to achieve a vision.

✓ Feature-driven companies can shift to sense and respond approaches, but this shift must be driven by leadership.

✓ Even large companies, governments, regulated industries, and safety-critical projects can use and are using sense and respond methods.

✓ Procurement rules can be an obstacle, but organizations are revising procurement standards to work in this way.

✓ Even well-respected brands can adopt this approach.

✓ Sense and respond is not a fad. It's a natural response to the nature of modern work.

4

You Are in the
Software Business

You might be tempted at this point to look at what Amazon and other technology companies are doing in this arena and say, "Well, that's fine for them, but we're not a technology company. We don't have to worry about these organizational changes." But that's simply not true. Digital technology is moving into every dimension of the business world, and it's forcing every business to consider how it will respond. Every business is now, in one way or another, a software business.

Take a moment and consider your organization. Picture the product or service you offer. Think about the way it's made, the way it's procured, the way your customers buy it, the way your users consume it. Those processes are changing because of digital technology.

Think about the way you sell it. The way you market it. The way your staff is trained. The way you account for it. The way you pay your employees and your suppliers. The way you work with your partners. In every dimension of your business, you are seeing radical change. And the driver of this change is digital technology. Or, more specifically, the change is driven by what your competitors, your customers, your users, and, yes, even your employees are now able to do—and are doing—thanks to this technology.

Understanding How User Behavior Is Changing Industries

In the 1990s Amazon was perhaps the first company to create a major commercial advantage by employing user-generated content. By allowing customers to review products on its site, the company actively engaged in two-way conversations with its customers and provided a material advantage to other shoppers seeking to purchase products on the internet. Accessing this content gave customers a reason to choose Amazon over rival services. But in the past ten years, we've seen online reviews and other user-generated content become an overwhelming force of its own. It's changing industries.

Consider the high end of the cosmetics industry, which has, for years, relied on department store makeup counters as a critical sales channel. These counters fill an important need for customers. Customers can walk into a department store, sit down at the counter, and get valuable advice about the products that are for sale. They can understand which products suit their needs and get instructions from trained professionals about how to use them.

But this channel has been under huge pressure lately: YouTube—once largely the land of cat videos and funny home movies—has been reborn in multiple new ways, among them as an advice channel. YouTube has been flooded with how-to videos; a recent YouTube search for "makeup" returned nearly 8.5 million videos. And these results cover a huge range of topics—"Makeup Tutorial for Brown Eyes," "For Beginners," "For Black Women," "For Teenagers." As with anything on the internet, some of these videos are not very good, but others are excellent. In fact, the best producers become stars. According to an industry publication, YouTube users watch more than 120 million beauty videos *each day*.[1] Perhaps more remarkable, of the beauty content available on the site, the major brands control only 3 percent.

It's not because the brands haven't tried to create their own content. It's because users want to hear from other users. Perhaps the biggest star user is Michelle Phan. With YouTube as her primary platform, Phan has more than eight million subscribers, and more than 1.1 billion views of her 350 makeup tutorial videos. Phan started posting videos to YouTube in 2007. In 2010, makeup giant Lancôme began sponsoring Phan's videos and made her its "official video makeup artist." Even more impressive was Phan's 2013 partnership with Lancôme's parent company, L'Oreal, which created a new product line called "em by Michelle Phan."

Brands as well as retailers are feeling the impact of user-generated online content. According to a recent report on the sector by Ernst & Young, "Growth, profitability and customer loyalty to a brand will be difficult to sustain. The new generation of connected customers, with instant access to globally transparent pricing, product comparisons and the opinions of luxury-bloggers, will make it more challenging to justify and sustain the high pricing differentials crucial to a luxury strategy."[2]

Responding to Changes in Consumer Expectations and Consumption Patterns

As digital services have become mainstream they've changed our expectations as consumers. If we need to know something, we Google it. If we need to get somewhere, we Uber it. Need a change from stale hotels in a foreign city? Airbnb it. If we need to buy something,

Amazon can have it at our door in two days or, in some cities, within the hour. We consult experts like Michelle Phan via YouTube, Twitter, and Pinterest. Oh, and all of these services and products are available to us wherever we are, whenever we request them, via the cool blue glow of our smartphone screens.

Why are these services winning? It's because they're offering customers the value they seek, in a way that is deeply responsive to their needs. The technology, handled correctly, is so malleable that it allows service providers and content creators to not only offer service but also adjust it in nearly real time to the way customers are using the service, the demand they're generating, and the feedback they're creating.

This is a pivotal moment in the way we approach our interactions with our customers. The same technology that powers continuous learning in our organizations drives the real-time interactions our customers are coming to expect from our companies. If we don't respond by meeting their expectations, they will tap their way to another provider in less time than it takes to say *iPhone*.

Learning the Nespresso Lesson

We saw this new era of customer expectations demonstrated recently, when management legend Tom Peters took to Twitter to share his frustration with his new Nespresso coffee pod machine. As his 127,000 Twitter followers looked on, Peters went on a multitweet rant to complain about his frustrations with the product and service.

First, he tried to register the machine, a gift from his wife. (We felt a little bad for her, too.) Peters tweeted as follows.

> Boo! Hiss! Pathetic! Registering my new Nespresso machine harder than registering a car in MA

Five hours later, still frustrated, Peters continued.

> Nespresso registration tried again w/more info than would give
> CIA for security clearance. These folks truly are insanely awful/
> suckworthy.

Three more hours later, Peters challenged his followers to
a wager.

> Up for $1000 bet? I bet $1k that CEO of Nestle has never
> used his company's website to execute a practical customer
> task.[3]

The futile attempts of Nespresso's customer service Twitter team
to assuage Peters's concerns, once a private matter between customer and company, were no longer private. They were playing out
on Twitter, and the whole internet was watching. And to make mat-
ters worse, the story was picked up by the media and caused the
company even more embarrassment.[4]

Seeing Problems as Opportunities

It doesn't have to be this way. If you're listening to customers' feedback and watching their interactions with your service, you are in
a position to turn points of friction into valuable new customer
interactions—*before* a famous pundit notices and takes you down in
public. Take, for example, this small story from Spotify, an online
music-streaming service.

Spotify had a quirk in the way its service worked. Only one instance of an account could be streaming music at any given time. If
you listened to Spotify on your computer and then started listening on your phone, it would cut off the stream to your computer.
This wasn't a big problem for individual users, but it meant that

you couldn't share your account with your family; for example, they couldn't listen in the kitchen if you were listening in your car.

Customers complained, and Spotify was able to quantify the size of the problem by looking at service metrics. It was big. But was the problem one user using two devices, or was the problem that people were sharing accounts? The company needed to know more. Without much fanfare, and as part of its twice-monthly app updates, it introduced a feature that warned customers when another device was about to interrupt their stream and gave them the option to choose the next step. This change improved the customer experience, but it did more than that. It gave Spotify a new data collection (sensing) opportunity. Based in part on this new insight, it was able to observe the data and collect evidence to allow it to offer a new service: a "family" plan that, in exchange for a slightly higher monthly rate, allows concurrent streaming to members of the same household.

Responding to Customers: You're in the Software Business Now

These stories demonstrate two important concepts. The Spotify story demonstrates that if you understand what your customers are trying to do, you can probably find a way to create a valuable service for them—one they are willing to pay for. Nespresso's story illustrates our second concept: even tried and true business models like Nespresso's (sell the coffee machine and then continue to make money by selling customers the coffee pods the machine requires) are now multichannel services. Nespresso customers buy their coffee pod refills online, so guess what? Nespresso is in the software business. It's not enough to have great machines that look good and make delicious coffee. Nespresso has to get that service right, too.

Using Multichannel Services: Sonic Automotive

Responding to consumer feedback is no longer optional. Ignoring customer feedback means not only risking loss of sales but also losing your ability to drive the narrative about your business. This is particularly true in the auto sales industry.

Before the mass adoption of the internet, car buyers typically visited multiple dealerships before making a buying decision. Now it's down to an average of 1.9 dealership visits prior to a sale. Customers do the bulk of their research online. They check inventory, make price comparisons, and read reviews of customer service.[5] Customers enter the dealership informed about the vehicle they want to buy, from its features to the "right" price to pay for it. And they're prepped in terms of the type of service to expect from each dealer. Dealerships know they have a bad reputation for service, and they know their customers are better informed now than ever before. Given all that, dealerships themselves are turning to technology to address these digitally empowered customers.

Sonic Automotive, a *Fortune* 500 company and one of the largest US automotive dealership conglomerates, has been sensing the ongoing shifts in car buyer behavior for years. The company tracks customer interactions through every channel—on the web, through its mobile apps, and, more recently, through its in-store interactions. To better serve the showroom customers who are ready to walk to the next dealership in the blink of an eye, Sonic armed its salespeople with iPads that help ensure immediate access to inventory details, customers' stated preferences, and downstream services such as financing and insurance. This gives salespeople the ability to respond to the customers who do choose their dealership in a way that competitors can't. The goal here is to increase the credibility of the salesperson by making her more responsive to specific queries and giving her the ability to complete a sale without the dreaded "hand-off to the finance guy" piece of the process.

Weaving digital tools into a traditional sales process is important, but the goal is to create satisfied customers. So, in addition, Sonic has changed another key component of its service offering: the compensation structure. It is shifting away from a commission-only compensation model, which the company believes drives the adversarial relationship between buyer and salesperson. Now, salesperson compensation is 75 percent base salary and a 25 percent bonus that is based on customer reviews. All of a sudden, a salesperson's goal is not to sell the most cars but to provide the best customer experience. Online comments, reviews, ratings, and other forms of user-generated content drive Sonic's assessment of that customer experience. The dividends this pays can then be quantified in sales, repeat sales, online reviews, and word-of-mouth marketing.

Although many of the stories we've shared have focused on digital service enhancements, it's important to remember that digital isn't a goal in and of itself. The goal is to drive some kind of change and add some kind of value. In other words, Sonic's iPad initiative isn't about iPads. It's about service. Digital tools simply give Sonic a way to measure the service-related outcomes it is trying to achieve. By concentrating on user-generated content, Sonic is engaging in the kind of two-way conversation with the market that sense and respond is all about.

Seeing Consumer Pressure in Other Industries

The pressure of the digital consumer reaches across industries. It's probably no surprise to see this dynamic play out in consumer businesses like auto dealerships. But it is happening in niche industries as well, even in some of the oldest businesses in the world.

Animal breeding is a centuries-old practice, one that relies on a mix of direct experience with herds and wisdom handed down from generation to generation. However, younger farmers, taking over for the previous generation, are becoming increasingly tech-savvy. Thus, they're relying less on generational knowledge and more on Google. Why remember everything when you can just look it up?

Select Sires is a US company that serves dairy and beef producers. Based in Ohio, Select Sires is "the largest Artificial Insemination organization in North America."[6] Said another way, it sells bull semen to cattle farmers. Some customers breed cattle for meat, others for milk. These farmers reach out to Select Sires to help them grow their herds and maintain their herds' health and productivity generation after generation.

For Select Sires, competition in the space has grown dramatically. Due to increased intermixing of bull bloodlines, differentiation at the product level (the semen itself) is becoming difficult to achieve. If Select Sires produces a top animal, the buyer, usually an experienced animal breeder, can then use that bull to create a competing product. So Select Sires has to offer more than a good product.

It turns out that managing the genetics of a large herd is a complex, data-intensive operation. You need to build desirable traits across the herd, avoid inbreeding, and watch for patterns and weaknesses in the herd. For farmers with hundreds or thousands of animals, this can be incredibly challenging. And for Select Sires, it is where the opportunity for differentiation comes in.

In the 1960s, the early days of Select Sires operations, staff would rate animals in a herd on fifteen different characteristics, standing next to the animals and entering the information on a paper work sheet. Then breeders would sort through all that paper to find the right matches for breeding—a mating service. Over the years, data collection moved to handheld computers, and analysis became more sophisticated. Now, the company's younger, tech-savvy target market demands instant access to genetic details and comparison data.

To meet this demand, Select Sires has staffed up on software engineers. It has created a search service—think of it as Google for bovine breeders—coupled with a comparison database that allows buyers to see where the Select Sires product outshines the competition.

It has also created a digital version of its mating service. A customer can enter a set of desired traits he'd like to see in a future herd. For example, if the herd will produce milk for a cheese plant, a farmer can use Select Sires' web-based software tools to select these qualities and have results presented in a matter of seconds. A process that would have taken hours of paperwork now happens in an instant.

Select Sires uses the search data these digital services generate to improve its own offerings as well. It tracks and analyzes customer interactions with the systems in order to help assess market demand. Thus its product planning efforts are based on real evidence of customer behavior and needs, rather than guesswork and gut feeling about what farmers will want next season.

It's not only the customer-facing aspects of the business that are being digitized. Select Sires has brought technology into the warehouse that holds the product, allowing the pickers and packers to work more efficiently, more quickly, and with fewer errors than before the change. In the warehouse, product is held in containers the size of coffee straws, and these in turn are held in liquid nitrogen. In the early days, order fulfillment was based on paper orders and inventory lists, tiny labels and manual tracking systems. To help locate and select product, warehouse staff now navigate the warehouse with a cart that has a desktop computer and a couple of monitors. The next project is to get all this power into a mobile device.

What's true for Select Sires is true across industries. It's not only customers. It's not only products. It's not only services. It's not only operations. Steadily, and across the board, everything is becoming powered by software. What's impressive is the degree to which Select Sires has been able to adapt. It has reconfigured how it presents and sells its product. It has modernized data collection and built a service on top of it. It has improved operations. And team members continue to rethink the way they do business and how they leverage technology to deliver the highest value to their market.

Answering the Competitive Threat You Never Saw Coming

In *The Innovator's Dilemma,* Harvard professor Clayton Christensen describes disruptive innovations—by which he means innovations that change industries and create new markets—as often appearing initially as nonthreatening. It might be a teenager's makeup tutorial on YouTube. It's less functional than your flagship product. (Famously, Michelle Phan applied to work at a Lancôme makeup counter and was rejected due to lack of experience.)[7] It's of lower quality. It's a toy. As a result, companies dismiss the innovation as noise and move on. It's not until this "toy" starts gathering strong customer traction that the incumbents pay attention—by which point it's often too late.

Entrepreneurship is not new, and neither is disruptive innovation. What is new, now, is the dramatic rise in the power of technology and its corresponding decline in cost. This has given rise to an entire generation of entrepreneurs tinkering with their own toys. They have access to scale and reach that in the past would have taken years (and required massive investments) to create.

Technology has also increased the operating rhythm of these entrepreneurs. In the past, entrepreneurs might take years to bring their vision to market. Now an idea can be conceived, prototyped, and shipped to market for feedback in days. These fast-moving tests are easy to laugh off, until suddenly you find that they're a material threat to your core business. For repeated examples of this technologically fueled phenomenon, look no further than mass media journalism.

BuzzFeed Versus the New York Times: *It Seemed Like a Joke*

BuzzFeed launched in 2006 as a series of experiments to find the most shareable content on the web. Founder Jonah Peretti, at the helm of his other media startup, the *Huffington Post*, launched a side project focused on sifting through millions of links to find ones that resonated with mass audiences. Two years later, BuzzFeed was generating a million unique visitors per month, drawing them in with a mix of photo memes, catchy lists (like "21 Photos That Will Restore Your Faith in Humanity"), and sponsored content. Funding started to pour in, and the company grew.

Even though the content was trivial—and this is probably why mainstream media organizations ignored it—BuzzFeed was perfecting a new kind of distribution model, one powered by sharing. Experiment by experiment, BuzzFeed was learning. The features that survived on the site supported one action above all else: sharing. And it's that continuous sharing of content that has helped it grow to 150 million monthly unique visitors at the time of this writing.

BuzzFeed could have rested on its laurels and continued on the same trajectory, but five years into its existence it did something interesting. It took the platform and audience it had created and began to feed it legitimate news content. It hired veteran journalists who covered sports, politics, and national and international news events. As 2012 rolled around, traditional news outlets perked up. Their numbers were hurting. Where were the readers going? It turns out, they were going where they had always been going: to BuzzFeed. But this time, along with viewing the list of the thirty most adorable kittens in the world, they were reading about the presidential election cycle and other major news topics. The toy had become legit. In less than ten years, BuzzFeed had built an audience that was three times the size of the readership of organizations like the *New York Times* were seeing on their web properties.

This is the power of technology. It is not beholden to traditional business models or points of view. It's not limited by the physical production of goods or the geographical limitations of distribution. It can be leveraged for experimentation, conversation, and learning at a pace impossible without it. BuzzFeed is only one of the new media companies working this angle, but, make no mistake, it is happening in every industry.

Analyzing the New York Times' Response

By 2013, though, executives at the *New York Times* were certainly paying attention. Feeling the pressure of the digital revolution, they commissioned an internal audit—one that lasted six months (an eternity in internet years). The result of that audit was the March 2014 *New York Times Innovation Report*, a report intended for internal audiences but subsequently leaked online shortly after its delivery.[8] It's a document that we're all lucky to have. It's remarkable for its thoroughness, candor, and insight; it's a model that learning organizations can strive to copy.

It is also, not incidentally, an indictment of using traditional business practices to operate in a digital context, and it has lessons that apply broadly, beyond journalism. It's filled with tremendous insight into what to focus on as your company navigates toward the future.

The report opens this way:

> The *New York Times* is winning at journalism. Of all the challenges facing a media company in the digital age, producing great journalism is the hardest. Our daily report is deep, broad, smart and engaging—and we've got a huge lead over the competition. At the same time, we are falling behind in a second critical area: the art and science of getting our journalism to readers. We have always cared about the reach and impact of our work, but we haven't done enough to crack that code in the digital era.[9]

How does an organization built up over a century and a half to do business in a certain way suddenly shift its operating structure, incentives, organization chart, and delivery mechanisms to address these new challenges? Perhaps the best articulation of an answer in the report came from Audrey Cooper, the managing editor of the *San Francisco Chronicle*. Cooper is quoted as saying, "We hope to eventually get to the point where instead of being a newspaper company that produces websites, we think of ourselves as a digital company that also produces a newspaper."[10]

In many ways that quotation underpins the entire thesis of this book: you must see your organization as a digital company first. Your products and services live on top of that digital framework so that they can be broadly accessible and scalable while continuously improving to meet customers' expectations. The *Times* executives weren't evaluating their competitors on their digital strategies. They were comparing journalistic quality—a yardstick by which they were consistently winning. And yet the readership numbers reflected a different reality. This is perhaps the biggest takeaway from this story: even though the quality of your product may remain superb, the channels through which your customers consume it are in constant evolution. Those channels are increasingly digital, and although that may seem daunting if you don't work in a "technology" company, the power of building sense and respond conversations through these channels is equaled only by the risk of ignoring it.

In response to the report, the *Times* has taken significant steps toward unifying the digital and print sides of the house. You could see a hint of this at work on Oscar night 2014, when the paper tweeted a link to a 161-year-old *Times* story on Solomon Northup, whose memoir served as the basis for the movie *12 Years a Slave*, which won three awards that evening. And it has made changes in the newsroom—cutting off access to the desktop version of NYTimes.com to focus the staff on mobile and, more recently, sharing web analytics numbers with reporters. The latter is a controversial practice, but one designed to make everyone aware of the distribution challenges the paper faces. These changes, though risky, reflect the spirit of the report authors, who noted, "We must push against our perfectionist impulses. Though our journalism always needs to be polished, our other efforts can have some rough edges as we look for new ways to reach our readers."[11]

It appears to be working, at least for now. In the last report before this book went to print, the *Times* reported digital ad revenues were up 10.6 percent, and digital subscription revenues were up 13.3 percent.[12]

Adapting to the New Playing Field

We've said a couple of times that you're in the software business. We could just as easily have said that your competitors already are in the software business. This is because the new digital capabilities and practices we're describing have created a new playing field for all of us. Let's take a moment to look around at that playing field.

Improving Geographic Reach

If there's one thing the digital economy has clearly redefined, it's our ability to play on a global scale. There was a time when having global reach meant you needed offices and warehouses and people on every continent. That's no longer true.

No business embodies the new idea of scale more than Facebook, the archetype of twenty-first-century scale. With nearly 11,000 employees, it has a market cap of $257 billion. Compare that with General Electric, which has a similar market cap of $288 billion but more than 300,000 employees and offices in nearly every country on the planet. Wal-Mart, with a market cap of $212 billion, has more than 2.2 million employees.

Perhaps more remarkable, though, is Facebook's reach. Facebook boasts an unfathomable 1.6 billion (yes, with a *b*) monthly active users. Despite the fact that the bulk of its employees are based in California, nearly 83 percent of Facebook users are outside the United States. And the company is only twelve years old as of this writing. How could it have attained such global impact with so few employees and in such a short amount of time? The answer, of course, is software.

Gaining Multichannel Reach

To reach into people's lives, you simply need to exist digitally—on the web, in an app, on their devices. In fact, your customers expect you to be there. Increasingly, then, companies are moving into digital channels. Some seem like silly experiments, but others—the ones that create meaningful value for customers—quickly become essential.

Over the past few years, Domino's Pizza has been pushing aggressively into digital channel experiments. Its stores are found everywhere in the United States, but you may not be near one (or aware that one is near) when the pizza mood strikes. Domino's now integrates with at least eight digital channels. You can order via Twitter. You can order from your car using Ford's SYNC platform, or you can order from the Domino's mobile app. In fact, a recent development allows you to order pizza by simply texting a "pizza slice" emoji to your nearest Domino's restaurant. Domino's has never been known for having the best pizza, but clearly it's hoping that convenience and fun will attract and retain a loyal customer base. These might seem like toys, but remember the lessons of *The Innovator's Dilemma*: today's toys can become tomorrow's disruptive innovations.

Another brand that's weaving a multichannel experience out of digital fabric is fashion designer Rebecca Minkoff. At her flagship connected store in New York, the designer's staff uses RFID tags to track the movement of items in the store. When a customer brings an item into the dressing room, a special touch screen display integrated into the mirror "knows" that the item is there and turns the mirror into a display to show the item in other colors and to showcase complementary accessories. Shoppers can request a different size or color directly via the mirror device. Customers can also use it to order a free coffee or a glass of champagne by simply entering their phone number. And with this detail, Minkoff is able to close the loop by linking in-store behavior to an individual customer's online account. If the customer has been on the website and made a purchase or a built a wish list, the store can bring those items up on the mirror screen as well.

Minkoff's merchandisers also glean insight from the system. They are able to track what items get pulled into the dressing rooms, what gets left behind, and what gets purchased. In a sense, the entire store—offline as well as online version—is continuously responding to customer behavior and creating value for both the customer and the business.[13] This is still another example of the continuous conversation with customers that digital services enable.

Scaling User-Centered Value into Big Business

Why do these digital improvements and updated offerings drive loyalty and scale? It would be easy to answer by assuming that consumers are always after the newest, shiniest enhancement or gadget. The reality, though, is that responding to consumer needs improves the user experience and creates value.

It's not the technology itself. That's become commoditized and cheap. Instead, it's the value you offer to customers that creates the competitive advantage. If you can make a product easier to use, reduce the time it takes a customer to complete a task, or provide the right information at the exact moment it's needed, you win. This is what Uber does: it solves one small problem, the problem of hailing a cab, exceedingly well. And, with the ability of technology to give it global reach, it has upended the traditional taxi business and grown into fifty-eight countries and three hundred cities in only six years. Uber is expected to generate $10 billion in revenue in 2016 without owning a single vehicle. It's these user experience improvements that consumers pay for and share with their friends. It's these moments of delight—digital or not—that increase loyalty to your brand.

Using Platforms to Build Things Quickly

What enabled Michelle Phan, BuzzFeed, Uber, and countless other businesses to succeed and scale has been the proliferation of digital platforms. Platforms are everywhere. They form the foundation of the digital interactions we experience. You can think of them as building blocks—the parts and infrastructure pieces we combine to create digital products and services. This proliferation of platforms is interesting for a few reasons.

We don't have to do all the work

First, the systems that technology companies once had to build from scratch are now available from third parties. They're mature, stable, and getting better each day. So while once we might have had to build our own systems to manage the basics (customer log-in, payments, etc.), now we can outsource those tasks to others and focus on developing only the parts that are unique to our businesses.

They're cheap

There's been a proliferation of high-quality open source software that costs nothing to use. Platforms that are not open source typically have pricing that makes it very inexpensive to get started. Vendors often offer free or low-cost plans, charging more money only as you grow. This lowers the barrier to entry for everyone, giving three kids in a garage the same access to world-class tools that multinational corporations enjoy.

They offer vast and instant reach

We can use social media to start talking to customers around the globe. Anyone with a credit card can advertise on Facebook—it takes about fifteen minutes to buy a Facebook ad—and instantly reach an audience that's currently estimated at 1.6 billion people. We can create a blog on WordPress or open accounts on Pinterest, Tumblr, Instagram, and Snapchat and instantly reach millions of people.

What's more, e-commerce platforms like eBay and Etsy allow specialty retailers to emerge. When merchants outgrow those offerings, they can easily build their own e-commerce offerings with platforms like Shopify that allow them to set up an online store on their own website. Third-party payment processors can be integrated into the site by a software developer in a matter of minutes.

The basic infrastructure services we need are all available in the cloud. Amazon's web services division, AWS, now functions as the data center for a huge percentage of digital businesses. It has even added the US Central Intelligence Agency as a customer.[14] And, as with all of these platform providers, the barrier to entry is ridiculously low. You can start hosting your business on AWS with a credit card and a web browser, and grow from there.

They allow you to move quickly

What do all of these platforms have in common? They're software services built and designed to reduce the friction of doing business. They allow a team to go from idea to launch in only a few days; they make the ubiquitous MVP (minimum viable product) possible. They provide flexibility to scale up and down as dictated by business performance. They allow companies to focus on building only the parts of their systems that add value and turn to third-party providers for most of the rest of what they need. These are the great equalizers between the big corporation and the entrepreneurial duo in a garage. And although large companies undoubtedly have more-complex problems to solve, the competitive threat these platforms create by arming smaller firms is no less real.

Seeing What Your Customers Are Doing

The *New York Times* ran a story recently about a Nielsen family. The television ratings service has, for years, been the go-to source for media and advertising executives trying to understand what Americans are watching on TV. But Nielsen is still mailing paper surveys to the families it monitors. Even worse, according to the viewer the *Times* spoke with, there was no room on the paper survey for him to record the shows that he and his family streamed over Netflix. The family had been without cable TV for five years, but Nielsen had no systematic way to know that. Understandably, media executives are frustrated.[15]

You can bet, though, that streaming media providers like Netflix know exactly how many viewers are watching their shows. This is because digital streaming is built on top of software that reports back to Netflix on what people are watching. In other words, when you stream a show on Netflix, you're participating in a two-way conversation with the company that helps it understand your preferences. Recently, Netflix publicly shared some of these insights about Americans' streaming habits. For example, subscribers who binge watch an entire season of a show typically take about a week, dedicating at least two hours a day to the task. These are the statistics that Nielsen, with its paper-based process, is missing.

For Netflix, the ability to sense what its subscribers are doing fuels very specific responses. In a recent interview, Netflix chief content officer Ted Sarandos explained that Netflix doesn't think of ratings in the same way a traditional network might: "We may build a show for 2 million people and we may build a show for 30 million people." So it doesn't want to compare shows against each other. "That puts a lot of creative pressure on the talent that we don't want to."[16]

The point is that modern businesses that deliver services digitally have built-in data collection capabilities. (Mature data collection and analysis platforms make it relatively easy to build in this capability from the start.) They know what their customers are doing and can respond to that behavior quickly. They can make better-informed decisions in nearly real time. They no longer need to make big, risky guesses about what their customers want: they can sense it.

Understanding That the Limiting Factor Is Now Operational

Platforms offer mature, stable infrastructure from which you can build products and services that reach millions. These products generate insight, thanks to the data you can collect from your systems. So the final piece of the puzzle isn't really about technology. It's about people—specifically, the people in your organization. Are you set up in a way that allows you to respond? Can your speed of response match your speed of insight? We're not talking about how fast you can make things, but rather how fast you can *decide* to make things.

Changing the speed with which you can respond to new insight is all about decision making. These decisions must reflect the pace at which information flows in. To do that, an organization has to trust that its managers will make the right decisions. The people best positioned to make real-time decisions (i.e., to respond to incoming data) are the people actually making the product or carrying out the policy change. No one has a greater level of investment than these frontline execution staff. They're the closest to the market and are likely to have the greatest insight about how to respond. Companies that give these teams the freedom to respond quickly, without bureaucracy, enable a pace of work that unlocks all the technical capability available in our twenty-first-century market.

The most common way to organize teams so that they can respond quickly is to use agile methods. Agile methods promote team-level empowerment and decision making based on data. Unfortunately, many companies have adopted agile methods without really understanding why they are doing so. Often these methods are used simply to execute a predetermined plan. Decision making—the ability to respond to feedback from the market—remains outside the team, and thus operates at a much slower pace. This is the mindset of the industrial age, a mindset driven by the pursuit of perfection, lengthy production cycles, assembly lines, and long chains of command. It's also what will allow more-nimble competitors to capitalize on opportunities before you do. Instead, you must hand over control of the tactical decisions to the teams that are closest to this insight.

Empowering Your Employees

There's another set of expectations you'll need to meet if you want your business to scale—your employees'. Outside of work, employees are consumers, too. They use the same technology as everybody else. When they come to the office, all too often they're asked to work with dated technology or have access locked down by tight security restrictions. (If you know anyone who works on Wall Street, you probably know someone who carries two smartphones—one issued by the company, the other personal.) Requests for system purchases or enhancements have to run a gauntlet of approvals, budgetary sign-offs, and behind-the-scenes political maneuvering to get implemented.

Most employees come to work to do good work. To get around these obstacles and to get their jobs done, they sometimes work around the system—a phenomenon known as *shadow IT*, or the use of unapproved technology systems by employees to do company work. By some estimates this happens at 75 percent of companies. Although it's no surprise that system administrators are displeased by this phenomenon, there's reason to believe that most employees using these tactics are actually more productive at work. This is because the systems they're provided to do their jobs are simply inadequate. They're seeking the technology to do their jobs better. In other words, your employees want to take advantage of technology to be more productive, but corporate restrictions won't allow it.

Forcing employees to use poorly designed, slow, and unresponsive systems reduces their productivity and motivation. Just as many corporations are now supporting employees' use of personal devices for company work, so too must they now support external systems and technologies. But the need to modernize goes beyond the systems you allow people to use. It's also about allowing people to work with the technology in new ways.

Select Sires needed to hire software engineers for an industry historically defined by overalls and manure. Without modern systems and the freedom to exercise them, company leaders knew they would never attract, hire, and retain software developers. The same holds true for any company trying to hire digital talent: banks, pharmaceutical companies, newspapers, and retail organizations. Analyst Mary Meeker, in her "2015 Internet Trends Report," noted that 41 percent of millennials are likely to download applications to their phones or laptops to use for work, compared with 24 percent of older workers.[17] Empowering your workforce with technology is as important as ensuring you're meeting your consumers' evolving needs.

Comparing Narwhals and Orcas

As we consider the ways that we've all, perhaps unwillingly and perhaps unwittingly, found ourselves in the software business, it's worth taking a moment to consider a story of two teams, competing for high stakes, that took very different approaches to the problems and opportunities created by software.

It's not often that the real world behaves like sports: two teams, two approaches, one winner. But in 2012, we got a story just like that: Mitt Romney versus Barack Obama running for president of the United States.

Now we're not here to talk about politics or policy or left versus right. Instead, this is about fast-moving organizations dealing with the fundamental force of our time—digital technology. And it's a story of how the old, traditional approach to information technology got beaten—badly—by a new, integrated sense and respond approach.

Successful presidential campaigns in the United States are built on fund-raising, coordinating ground staff, and driving voter turnout. These days, those operations, and many more, are run through software systems—systems that the campaigns need to create. It's a big technological effort, and it happens in adverse, unpredictable conditions, and it all has to happen fast.

Running the Romney Campaign: Project Orca

On the surface, Romney's plan, a system code-named Orca, seems like what we all dream about when we imagine powerful computer systems. The Romney campaign imagined a comprehensive voter information system that would track all the voters in all the precincts in the country, allow volunteers to target critical voters in their districts, and reach out directly to them on Election Day to make sure that every possible Romney voter would get to the polls.

"We are going to know more than the exit polls will be able tell us," Romney campaign communications director Gail Gitcho told PBS. "At 5 o'clock when the exit polls come out, I doubt we will pay attention to it because we will have had much more scientific information."[18]

The Romney campaign was confident that its technology effort, run by some of the best firms it could hire, would be its secret weapon. "The Obama campaign likes to brag about their ground operation," Gitcho said, "but it's nothing compared to this."

Romney himself, in a campaign video about his technology program, said, "With state of the art technology . . . our campaign will have an unprecedented advantage on Election Day."[19]

They called the system Orca because orcas are the only known predator of narwhals—which happened to be the code name the Obama team had given to its system.

Running the Obama Campaign: Project Narwhal

The Obama campaign was, of course, working on its own software systems and had been for months before the election. The team members just weren't talking about it, at least not to the press. In fact, outside the campaign very little beyond the name was known about the effort.

But even though they weren't talking to the press, Obama's tech team (a team that was working in-house for the campaign) *was* talking to its volunteers. In fact, in the months running up to Election Day, the campaign was rolling out service after service to the volunteers—testing, refining, and continuously improving a broad range of services. It was, in effect, hiding in plain sight. And team members weren't simply building a get-out-the-vote tool but also fund-raising systems, volunteer coordination systems, and data analytics systems. They built clever voter engagement programs, too. The much-mocked Dinner with Barack campaign was actually the opener in a sophisticated two-way conversation that engaged voters, collected email addresses, and exemplified the kind of modern, ongoing sense and respond engagement that digital programs can create. In contrast, Romney's campaign didn't launch Orca until just before election day.

Winning Election Day

So how did it go? Election Day proved to be a disaster for Romney's Orca. The first warning signs were seen the night before, as Romney volunteers got their first look at the system. They were confused by hard-to-follow and incomplete instructions. They were dismayed that many of the operations were designed for smartphone users, when many of the volunteers were using plain old cell phones. In contrast, Obama's systems had the advantage of having been in use by volunteers for months. Those volunteers had been confused at the beginning, too—but the campaign had used their early feedback to improve the system continuously, so that by Election Day, everything was running smoothly.

On Election Day itself, Orca collapsed under early demand and remained down for most, if not all, of the day. The Romney digital team members, concerned with security, had chosen to keep the system under wraps and to operate out of one data center that they built themselves and located near Boston Garden, Romney's operations center for the day. As a result of this decision, the people who developed the system didn't have access to the Garden systems until just before Election Day. And the people who would operate the systems at the Garden were not the same people who developed the system. There was going to have to be a hand-off, and the two teams would have only one shot to get it right. They had no time to get up to speed and would have little time to recover if there was a problem. Zac Moffatt, Romney's digital director, later said, "The primary issue was we beta-tested in a different environment than the Garden."[20] In other words, the team never tested under real-world conditions and never built the kind of collaboration that could overcome this problem.

Obama's team went a different direction. The campaign built a different kind of team that had tight integration between the developers and operations teams. They weren't working at separate firms; they all worked together from the beginning of the project. Together, the team members built and tested a system that was robust and failure resistant. They didn't use a single data center; instead, they ran their system on Amazon's cloud service and were able to build, test, and adjust the system from day one right up until Election Day.

In short, Obama's systems decisively beat Romney's. Did that decide the election? There is some controversy about this. But the race was tight, and some observers estimate that as many as thirty thousand Romney volunteers in critical districts were idled because of the failure of the Romney systems. Whether or not the system failure decided the election, it would be hard to argue that Romney's team made good choices in terms of digital operations.

Knowing What the Obama Team Knew

Mitt Romney is an experienced strategist. He is a veteran of the management consulting world in the 1970s and 1980s—an alum of The Boston Consulting Group and a former partner at Bain & Company—before entering politics. He knows how to manage large organizations. But in his 2012 campaign, at least, he was working from an old playbook when it came to technology.

The Obama team had reason to think its approach was better than Romney's: the Obama team members themselves had tried four years earlier to do much of what the Romney team tried in

2012. And it didn't work for them then either. So, learning from their technology failures in the 2008 campaign, the Obama team members chose a completely different approach. Instead of making big plans, they went small. Instead of a big bang launch, they rolled out small pieces over time. Instead of working in secrecy and isolation, they worked collaboratively across functions and departments.

They knew how to do this, in part, because of what the software industry in general has learned in the past ten years. The Obama campaign assembled a crack team of technology people at the headquarters in Chicago, many of whom had left their jobs in Silicon Valley to work on what was essentially a hot new startup—the Obama campaign, called Obama for America. These people, immersed in the culture of Silicon Valley, were able to bring the most modern methods to the campaign.

Understanding Why "Software Is Eating the World"

In 2011, legendary technology entrepreneur Marc Andreessen shared his conviction that "software is eating the world." His case is one we agree with, and one that we've summarized here. It's an important position, and one that's been widely quoted.

But as important as it is, the implications of Andreessen's observation are just now being felt broadly across industry. Organizations that have been built on older, industrial methods must now confront the disruptive forces of software, and they must do so by taking up a new playbook we've described here in Part I. In Part II, we dig into the details of the playbook and explore the implications for managers in every part of the organization.

Sense and Respond Takeaways for Managers

✓ Increasingly, all organizations will have to confront the disruptive power of software.

✓ Software is changing not only the products and services you deliver but also the way you operate your business.

✓ Software is changing the market's expectations of your business, empowering your competition, and enabling new competitors.

✓ To survive and thrive, your organization must recognize that the old management playbook needs to be replaced by a new one.

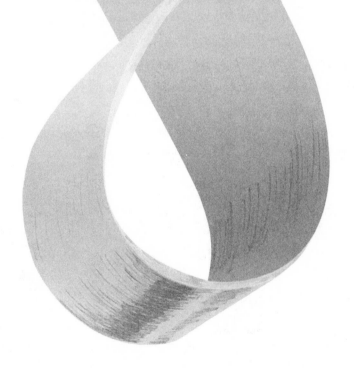

PART TWO

A Manager's Guide to Sense and Respond

5

Plan for Change and Uncertainty

When is work finished? For most of us, it seems pretty simple: it means getting our work done. We learn this early in our school lives: finish your homework. Do your chores. When you're done, you get to stop working, get to play with your friends, read your books, watch a movie, and so on. We take this idea into our workplaces: finish that report. Do your rounds. Go to a meeting. When you're done? "Quittin' time!"

But we need to take a step back and consider what "done" really means. Does it mean that we've shipped a product or launched a service? Does it mean that it's making money for the company? Oddly, usually not. It's usually a few steps back from that. Sometimes it means, "We've built the thing you specified in the contract." Or sometimes it means, "We've written software, tested that it works, and deployed it to a server."

Usually, though, it doesn't mean, "We've finished making something that we know adds value to the business."

This is an important distinction, and we need to be clear about the differences. Most teams in business work to create a defined output. But creating an output is not the same as being successful. Just because we've finished making a thing doesn't mean that thing is going to create value for us. If we want to talk about success, we need to specify the target state we seek. Let's call that desired success an outcome.

For example, we may ask a vendor to create a website for us. Our goal might be to sell more of our products online. The vendor can make the website, deliver it on time and on budget, even make it beautiful to look at and easy to use, and it may still not achieve our goal, which is to sell more of our products online. The website is the output. The project may be "done." But if the outcome—sell more products—hasn't been achieved, then we have not been successful.

This may seem rather obvious, but if you look at the way most companies manage digital product development, you'd be hard-pressed to see these ideas in action. That's because most companies manage projects in terms of outputs and not outcomes. This means that most companies are settling for "done" rather than doing the hard work of targeting success.

Defining Done as Successful

Do companies really manage for *done* instead of *success?* And if so, why would they do that?

It turns out that there are some situations when these ideas are the same thing or have such a clear and well-understood relationship that they might as well be the same thing. This is frequently the case in industrial production. Because of the way industrial products are designed and engineered, you know that when your production line is spitting out Model T's, you can be reasonably certain they will work as designed. And, because of years of sales history, you can be reasonably certain that you will be successful: you will sell roughly the number of cars you forecast. Managers working in this context can be forgiven for thinking that their job is simply to finish making something.

With software, however, the relationship between *we're finished building it* and *it has the effect we intended* is much less clear. Will our newly redesigned website actually encourage sharing, for example, or will the redesign have unintended consequences? It's very difficult to know without building and testing the system. And—in contrast with industrial production—we're not making many instances of one product. Instead, we're creating a single system—or set of interconnected systems that behave as one system—and we are often in the position of not knowing whether the thing we're making will work as planned until we're "done."

In Uncertainty, Specifying Output Doesn't Work

This problem of uncertainty, combined with the nature of software, means that managing our projects in terms of outputs is simply not an effective strategy in the digital world. And yet, our management culture and our management tools are set up to work in terms of outputs. To consider one example, let's look at how companies typically purchase software from a third-party vendor.

In a typical process, we might commission an internal team to develop a request for proposal (RFP). This RFP would be based on some analysis of the business problem, would specify the nature of the solution and provide a list of requirements—typically features of the system—and request that vendors submit proposals.

Based on the RFP, vendors will submit proposals, typically specifying how they will go about building the solution: how long it will take, who will work on it, how much it will cost, and, of course, why the vendor is uniquely suited to doing this work.

Once we select a vendor, we then write a contract based on (1) the requirements we developed and (2) the price and time line that the vendor promised. When we sign the contract, both parties are committed to a project based on output. The vendor is committed to building a set of features—in other words, being *done*—rather than committed to creating something successful.

Identifying the Problem with Output

Of course, if you've purchased custom software with a process like this, you know what happens in this scenario. The vendor does not deliver as promised. Why? One veteran IT manager put it this way: "The problem is fixed-price contracts," he told us. "Both of you are fooling each other that you understand the problem." As a result, then, everyone must adjust when the true nature of the problem becomes clear. The result of the adjustments? The vendor is late or over budget. This IT veteran continued, "There's always a problem at the end, and, instead of solving the problem or improving the product, you end up fighting about who is going to pay for it."

Using the Alternative to Output: Outcomes

The old cliché in marketing is true: customers don't want a quarter-inch drill; they want a quarter-inch hole. In other words, they care about the end result and don't really care about the means. The same is true for managers: they don't care how they achieve their business goals; they just want to achieve them.

In the world of digital products and services, though, uncertainty becomes an important player and breaks the link between the quarter-inch drill and the quarter-inch hole. Some managers try to overcome the problems caused by uncertainty by planning in increasingly greater detail. This is the impulse that leads to detailed requirements and specification documents, but, as we've come to understand, this tactic rarely works in software.

It turns out that this problem—the way our plans are disrupted by uncertainty, and the fallacy of responding with ever-more-detailed plans—is something that military commanders have understood for hundreds (if not thousands) of years. They've developed a system of military leadership called *mission command*, an alternative to rigid systems of leadership that specify in great detail what troops should do in battle. Instead, mission command is a flexible system that allows leaders to set goals and objectives and leaves detailed decision making to the people doing the fighting. Writing in *The Art of Action*, Stephen Bungay traces these ideas as they were developed in the Prussian military in the 1800s and describes the system that those leaders developed to deal with the uncertainty of the battlefield.[1]

Mission command is built on three important principles that guide the way leaders direct their people:

- Do not command more than necessary, or plan beyond foreseeable circumstances.

- Communicate to every unit as much of the higher intent as is necessary to achieve the purpose.

- Ensure that everyone retains freedom of decision within bounds.

For our purposes, this means that we would direct our teams by specifying the outcome we seek (our intent), allowing for our teams to pursue this outcome with a great deal of (but not unlimited) discretion, and expecting that our plans will need to be adjusted as we pursue them.

Managing with Outcomes

Let's look at an example of how one team we worked with put these principles to work. In 2014, Taproot Foundation wanted to create a digital service that would connect nonprofit organizations with skilled professionals who wanted to volunteer their services. Think of it as a matchmaking service for volunteers. Taproot Foundation had to work with outside vendors and ended up choosing our firm for the project.

In our early conversations, Taproot leaders described the system that they wanted to build in terms of the features of the system: it would have a way for volunteers to sign up, it would have a way for volunteers to list their skills, it would have a way for nonprofit organizations to look up volunteers based on these skills, it would have a contact system for organizations to reach out to volunteers, it would have a scheduling system to allow the parties to arrange meetings, and so on. We were concerned about this feature list. It was a long list, and although each item seemed reasonable, we thought we might be able to deliver more value faster with a smaller set of features.

To shift the conversation away from features, we asked, "What will a successful system accomplish? If we had to prove to ourselves that the system was worth the investment, what data would we use?" This conversation led to some clear, concrete answers. First of all, the system needed to be up and running by a specific date, about four months away. The foundation participates in an annual event to celebrate the industry, and executives wanted to have a demonstrated success they could show off to funders at that event. We asked, "What does *up and running* mean?" Again, the answers were concrete: we need to have X participants active on the volunteer side, and Y participants active on the organization side. Because the point of the service would be to match volunteers with organizations so that they could do projects together, we should have made Z matches, and a certain percentage of those matches should have yielded successful, completed projects.

This was our success metric: X and Y participants; Z matches; percent of completed projects. (We actually set specific numerical targets, but for this telling, we're using variables.)

Next we asked, "If we can create this system and achieve these targets without building any of the features in your wish list, is that OK?" This was a harder conversation.

The executives signing the contract were understandably concerned: what guarantee did they have that we would complete the project?

This is the bind that executives and managers face: as they negotiate with partners, they are bound to protect their organizations. They need to find contractual language that ensures the partners will deliver. The problem with contracts, though, is that to make them work, managers are forced to settle for the protection they find in the concrete language of features: you build feature A, and we will pay you amount B. But this linguistic certainty is a false hope. It guarantees only that your vendor will get to "done," as in, "The feature is done." It does not guarantee that the set of features that you can describe in a contract will make you successful. On the other side, vendors are understandably hesitant to sign up to achieve an outcome, mostly because vendors rarely control all of the variables that contribute to project success or failure. Thus, both sides settle for a compromise that offers the safety of "done" while at the same time creating constraints that tend to predict failure rather than create the freedom that breeds success.

Our contract with Taproot, then, contained not only a list of desired features but also a list of desired outcomes. Here are the outcomes we wrote into the contract:

> The system will connect volunteers to organizations [at the following rate]. It will allow these parties to find each other, complete the communications needed to decide to work together, complete projects together, and report on the success of those projects. It will do so at [the following rates] and by [the following date]. If at any time, the team decides together that the desired outcomes are better served by building a different set of features than the desired features listed above, they may do so.

This language is a paraphrase—there was more legalese—but this was the essence of the agreement. This compromise—listing the features we thought were important, but being clear about outcomes and agreeing in advance that outcomes are more important—is the key to managing with outcomes instead of output.

It's worth acknowledging here that many organizations have little flexibility in terms of project funding processes and procurement rules, so this type of contract may be out of reach for some managers. But as we discuss in chapter 3, forward-thinking organizations are working from within to change that.

Seeing Results

So how did the project play out? First, the team decided that the most important milestone was to get the system up and running. Rather than wait four months—the length of the project—to launch, the team members decided to launch as quickly as possible. As it turned out, they were able to go live to a pilot audience within about one month. They launched a radically simplified version of the service, one with very few automated features. Most of the work in the system was done by a person, a community manager, playing a behind-the-scenes role.

(This is the same approach used by the Cooking Light Diet team, which we describe in chapter 2.)

This concierge minimum viable product (MVP) approach has become a popular way to launch systems. The Taproot team knew it would need more automation if it wanted the system to scale, but it also knew automation could come later. Launching early achieved two goals. First, it ensured that the team would have something to show to funders at the annual event. This was a hugely important marketing and sales goal. But launching early addressed an even more important goal: it allowed the team to learn what features it would *actually* need in order to operate the system at scale. In other words, it allowed the team to establish the sense and respond loop—the two-way conversation with the market that would guide the growth of the service.

The project planners had imagined, for example, that the skilled volunteers would need to be able to create profiles on the service. Organizations would then browse the profiles to find volunteers they liked. This turned out to be exactly wrong. When the team tried to get volunteers to make profiles, they responded with indifference. The team realized that, in order to make the system work, volunteers had to be motivated to participate; they needed to find projects that they were passionate about. In order to do this, the system needed project listings, not volunteer listings. In other words, the team had to reverse the mechanics of the system, because the initial plans were wrong.

By the second month of the project, the team had built the system with the revised mechanics and then concentrated on tuning the system: identifying the details of the business processes needed and building software to support those processes. How would the team make it easy for organizations to list their projects? How would team members make sure the listings were motivating to volunteers? How simple could they make the contact system? How simple could they make the meeting scheduler? At the end of the four-month project, the team had a system that had been up and running for three months and that far exceeded the performance goals written into the contract.

Solving the Local Knowledge Problem

Projects like this work because they follow the principles of mission command. They give teams a strategy and a set of outcomes to achieve, along with a set of constraints, and then give them the freedom to use their firsthand knowledge of the situation to solve the problem. In this case, the strategy that Taproot Foundation was pursuing was to use the power of the internet to increase the organization's impact by a factor of 10. The strategic constraints for the project were clear as well: funders had paid for the team to create an online matching service. No matter what the team did, it would have to produce an online matching service, although it had considerable freedom to define what that service would look like. The team also had a hard constraint in the form of a date: the system had to be up and running by a date four months in the future. But again, the team had considerable freedom to decide the definition of *up and running*.

This approach to project leadership is not common, but we see it more frequently on startup teams and in smaller organizations. Indeed the Taproot project was delivered by a single small team working with little need to coordinate with others. Scaling this approach to multiple teams and to larger organizations is a difficult and subtle problem, one that requires careful balance between central planning and decentralized authority.

We have seen many examples in the modern era of the failure of central planning. One only need look at the failures of the Soviet bloc and late-twentieth-century communist Chinese economies to find examples of what economists call the *local knowledge problem*: the idea that central planners don't have sufficient understanding of the tactical reality on the ground to make detailed plans. How much bread should go to this town? How much wheat should be allocated to this factory? What if there's a bad crop? What if the storage facility has a fire? What if the region is a rice-eating region?

The opposite of central planning is decentralized authority. At the extreme end of this decentralized spectrum are systems like anarchy, holocracy, and even, in some eyes, agile software development.

Agile does indeed put a great deal of stock in allowing small, egalitarian teams to make decisions. At a small scale, this resembles systems like anarchy, with their radically inclusive visions. But anarchy and holocracy make claims about how their systems scale; holocracy advocates claim that you can run large organizations without traditional hierarchies. Agile has, until recently, made no such claims. This idea—that agile has mostly ignored organization-scale problems and focused on team-level problems—was captured nicely by technology consultant Dan North. In a conference talk in 2013, North described it this way.

> Agile doesn't scale. There, I said it. Actually people have been telling me that for over ten years, and I've just refused to believe them, but they were right. Does that mean you can't deliver large-scale programmes using agile methods? Not at all.
>
> But to scale you need something else, something substantively different, something the Agile Manifesto and the existing team-scale agile methods don't even have an opinion about.[2]

Managing at the Program and Portfolio Levels

In the Taproot story, you saw how a single team can approach a project with agile methods. But if we truly want to create agile *organizations*, then we need to consider how agility applies not only at the team level but also at two additional levels above the team. First is the *program* level: a group of two or more teams working in coordination to achieve a shared goal. The second is the *portfolio* level: the collection of all the work in an organization.

In recent years, agile has moved from being a cultlike movement to being a mainstream way of working. (A recent report commissioned by Hewlett-Packard estimated that more than 90 percent of large IT organizations are either primarily using agile approaches or making significant use of them.)[3] And as agile methods have become mainstream, organizations around the world are trying to find solutions to making agile scale. This is because, as North indicates, agile is essentially a "team-scale" method of working, and large organizations need a system to coordinate the work of many teams.

One of the more popular approaches to this coordination is something called a *scaled agile framework*, or SAFe. As implied by the acronym, SAFe provides managers with a measure of comfort. After all, a huge organization filled with self-guided teams is a scary idea for managers. It sounds a lot like anarchy.

SAFe is a way of decomposing large projects into smaller pieces, assigning those pieces to teams, and creating accountability to ensure that teams complete the work that they've signed up to complete. The problem with this approach is that it is essentially a "more detailed plan" approach, and it ignores the influence of uncertainty. SAFe moves teams away from a sense and respond approach and toward a central-planning approach. In effect, it reduces the agile team to a production team, giving them a fixed set of requirements and expecting a specific output to emerge from the end of the assembly line. This approach can be appropriate for high-certainty efforts, but it limits an agile team's ability to learn from feedback as it goes forward. And again, it's this learning from feedback that allows teams to navigate in high-uncertainty contexts.

Instead of trying to fit agile into a command and control framework, we've seen many organizations adopt coordination approaches that are more in line with mission command—that move away from planning with outputs and toward managing with outcomes. These approaches use different tactics to coordinate the effort of large teams, but they tend to create something we call outcome-based road maps.

Using Outcome-Based Road Maps

Outcome-based road maps take many forms. We look at a few in the coming section, but before we do, let's consider their key elements. Outcome-based road maps work because they help create a multi-team implementation of mission command. They are a way of articulating, in a cascading manner, the key elements we need when we direct the work of teams:

- The strategic intent ("We want to increase the organization's impact by a factor of 10")

- The strategic constraints ("We will do this by creating an online matching service that must be live by X date")

- The definition of success ("The service will match parties at X rate")

When implemented well, outcome-based road maps help organizations create alignment, which is critical to making mission command work.

Bottom-Up Meets Top-Down Communication

There is a critical component of mission command that goes beyond simply *what* you communicate. Just as important is *how* you communicate it. Orders must be briefed up and down the chain of command; in other words, the communication and conversation must go in both directions, and this briefing up and down is ongoing. It's *continuous*. It is the process of communicating this way that creates alignment.

In researching this book, we learned about a company that was putting these methods to work as part of its annual planning process. This firm, an e-commerce startup based in the United States, is one of the more successful organization-wide practitioners of agile methods. It's not a by-the-book agile firm. Instead, it embodies many of the ideals and practices that are at the heart of agility. Among other things, it was an early and successful adopter of what is now called *continuous deployment*—the idea that software is not released every few months, or even every few weeks, but instead is released continuously. (We talk about this in chapter 1. It's the process by which Amazon is able to release software every 11.6 seconds.) Over the years, they have developed a culture around experimentation, A/B testing, and optimization.

The agile methods it implemented made it possible to take an experimental approach to releasing new software. Let's say, for example, it wants to redesign a product page on its website. Rather than guess which page performs better, it quickly designs and builds a few versions of the page, releases them to the site, directs a small, carefully controlled set of users to each version, and then measures which page performs best.

This experiment-based approach, because it is easy to do and because it yields powerful results, has quickly became a core element of the company's culture. It is normal for teams to work in this manner, continuously testing and optimizing their work a little at a time. But one manager told us that in the past, it became a problem: "We were focusing on quick wins, rather than program-building." The problem seems to have been in choosing what to test and, more generally, what to work on. When the company was smaller, it was easier to align the work of teams through informal means. But as it grew, more coordination was needed.

By the end of 2015, the company had grown to more than five hundred people and was generating hundreds of millions of dollars in annual revenue. The coordination problem was becoming acute. Executives knew they needed to create more alignment and better coordinate their activities. To do so, they put in place a top-down plus bottom-up planning effort in order to create a road map for the year.

Building an Outcome-Based Road Map

The first part of the work involved senior leaders, who created a list of strategic themes for the coming year. These themes would be the top-down guidance—the coordinating ideas that would serve as the rudder for the ship. Strategy is about choices. It's as much about what you don't do as what you choose to do. So for this year, following a period of intense focus on one segment of customers, the executives chose to focus on a different segment, one they felt had been underserved previously. From this focus, the leaders created a number of smaller themes, including a focus on the mobile experience. (Stephen

Bungay points out that a good strategy statement often "looks banal" to outsiders. The value comes from the alignment you create through the continuous process of articulating the strategy.)[4]

With the top-down strategic themes prepared, all the delivery teams were asked to create a list of initiatives they wanted to work on in the coming year. This was the bottom-up part of the process. The list came from the front line, the cross-functional team members who knew the most about the product, the customers, and the users. These were expert, informed opinions, deeply rooted in the situation on the ground. The teams also had to provide an estimate of the specific, measurable business outcomes they believed each initiative would create.

Next, the product leaders in the middle management layer needed to figure out how to coordinate the effort—in other words, how to create the road map for the year. The leads of the product teams came together to organize the wish list of initiatives. They grouped the initiatives in terms of which themes each project supported and then stack-ranked them in terms of the contribution they believed each initiative would have—that is, they associated each initiative with the outcome they thought the work would create and showed how those outcomes would support the strategic goals expressed by leadership. They estimated head count for each initiative and sent the results to the finance experts, who correlated these plans with some of the major financial metrics they tracked and considered how the proposed work might impact results. When this was done, the plan was sent back up to the executives for review.

The executive review of the proposed plan now faced what could be thought of as an editorial review by the executive team. The assessment? The plan was close but not ready. When the executives reviewed the plan, they realized they had missed an important feature they had promised the market, so they added that. They made a few adjustments and crossed some things off the list, and then they were ready with the road map.

This is an example of what we consider an outcome-based road map. It neatly ties the work you're planning to the outcomes you believe the work will have, and it ties the outcomes you seek to the strategic objectives you are trying to achieve. It creates a coherent story that connects the leadership of the organization to the troops on the ground.

One manager at the company told us, "The best companies have a 'product editor.' They have a story. If you look at Apple, they have a story, a narrative. With this approach, we have a story. As a product lead, I love this. I have direction."

Assessing the Cultural Impact

For this young company, this planning process was new; it replaced a different process it had used the year before, and still a different process from the year before that. So change was normal, but that doesn't mean everyone liked it. Most of the managers appreciated the clarity as well as the flexibility to pursue their initiatives. And other product teams appreciated the clearly defined negative space: "We don't have to work on *that* initiative, because it's not on the road map." But of course there were some hurt feelings, too. People didn't like proposing initiatives that didn't make the cut. Still, on balance, the process seems to have been a big step forward compared with earlier planning efforts.

Let's review some of the elements that made this process successful and, at the same time, consider how it supports the sense and respond approach that this company embodies.

- *Strategy is expressed as intent.* Rather than lay out a detailed plan, leadership set direction and asked the folks close to the customer to figure out the details.

- *Situational awareness defines tactics.* The staff members have a deep knowledge of what the real-world conditions are, what they'd like to fix, and what is realistic. They were able to select the best tactics to achieve the mission.

- *Commitments are made to outcomes rather than features.* By tying initiatives to outcomes rather than to features, leaders gave staff members the flexibility to pursue their missions and use their best judgment to achieve the desired outcomes.

- *A mix of bottom-up and top-down planning provides balance.* Unlike previous years, in which bottom-up planning resulted in a lack of coordination—or, as we see in many organizations, top-down planning creates a lack of flexibility—this process balanced inputs to create a healthy equilibrium.

Using Outcome-Based Road Maps at GOV.UK

The bottom-up meets top-down approach has also been part of the road mapping effort at GOV.UK., the official government website of the United Kingdom. The teams working on this site have been part of a pioneering effort to rebuild the online presence of the national government. The work being done there gives us a unique opportunity to study modern digital methods because of the project's unwavering commitment to openness.

Writing about the road mapping process, Neil Williams, a product lead at the UK's Government Digital Service, said, "Probably the toughest challenge in road mapping on a large, multiteam product is striking the right balance between (top-down) business goals and (bottom-up) team priorities."[5]

To align teams and strike this balance, the GDS uses what it calls "mission statements." Mission statements give "broad direction and boundaries to a problem space" that each team owns. This information provides strategic direction, guidelines about the constraints teams must observe, and, at the same time, the autonomy for teams to find the best solution to the problem they've been given. Mission statements function similarly to the strategic goals and outcomes that you saw the e-commerce startup use in its road mapping process. By aligning around missions, the GOV.UK road map is yet another type of outcome-based road map.

The road map also has to strike a balance between making specific promises and allowing flexibility in both time commitments and features to be delivered. In other words, it has to communicate clearly what teams intend to do and, at the same time, allow for plans to change and evolve in response to learning.

The team uses a combination of tactics here. First, team members are conscientious about time promises. And second, they try to limit making hard commitments to anything except the most near-term work.[6] They slice the future into three buckets. During "current" work, which looks ahead about a month, they make relatively firm commitments as to what they'll deliver. Next comes "planned" work, which is one to three months away from being started, and work that is being considered but is not confirmed. Finally, there is a longer-term bucket called "prioritized" work. This is work that is tentative.[7]

You should be able to see in this approach one of the central tenets of mission command: do not command more than necessary or plan beyond circumstances you can foresee.

Author Donald Reinertsen, who studies lean methods, has this to say about planning and alignment: "The modern military does not create plans for the purpose of measuring conformance; they plan as a tool for maintaining alignment."[8] Indeed, Williams told us the goal at GOV.UK is to create "aligned autonomy."

The importance of alignment is visible in the GOV.UK project's commitment to openness. All of its road maps are available for internal teams, stakeholders, and the public. The team uses a variety of tools to create this visibility: a huge physical poster wall in its office, an official and active blog available on the open web, and a web-based road map hosted in a tool called Trello.[9] All of this visibility is an attempt to create alignment among teams, stakeholders, and the public.

Planning with a Customer-Centered Perspective

At Westpac, the oldest bank (in fact the oldest company) in Australia, the customer experience team has been applying something called customer journey mapping to create alignment for multiteam initiatives and programs.

A *customer journey map* is a big chart—at Westpac they are usually wall-sized charts composed of many sheets of paper—that shows the end-to-end journey customers complete as they interact with a business. For example, what's the process for getting a credit card? Or of taking out a home loan? A business process like this is complicated and requires many teams to contribute. It touches many bank systems, from web and mobile apps to in-house systems used in the branches, in the call centers, and in the back office. The people creating and using these systems need to be working with some alignment if they hope to deliver good service to customers. The journey map is the focus of a larger "program design wall" that is intended to create alignment across all of these teams.

The customer experience team actually creates two journey maps for each process and puts them on the wall together. The first, what the team calls the *As Is* (or *current state*) map, shows the current process the customer navigates, warts and all. In fact, calling out pain points, bottlenecks, and inefficiencies is the entire point of the As Is map.

Then the team works with stakeholders to create a second version of the map—this one is a *vision of the future*. It's a vision that will be better for the bank and for customers, because it eliminates the obstacles they currently face and delivers more value. For example, the team recently completed work on a vision to improve how customers are issued credit cards: the As Is version showed a process that takes five days or more for customers to complete. In the vision of the future it takes five *minutes*. The benefit to customers is obvious, but the benefit to the bank also is important. A better process will yield more customers and will get them active and using the credit card sooner.

Avoiding Feature-Based Road Maps

The Westpac team found that it took it a while to get the vision maps right. Team members had to create a compelling story (and thus generate excitement and alignment) but avoid being too detailed. They didn't want to lock in too soon on features that might not work. In other words, they wanted to preserve each team's freedom of action—the team's ability to own, or at least participate in, creating the right solution. Ian Muir, head of customer experience, told us, "The key is finding the right balance when you're telling the story of the future and you don't have all the information you want."

With the two journey maps on the design wall, next comes the planning phase. At this point, it's about getting the delivery teams into the room to review the map themselves. The teams have already been part of the process of creating the maps, but now the next step is to figure out how to deliver the experience they've helped imagine. This step is when self-direction and multiteam coordination meet. Dan Smith, a customer experience manager, says, "I tell them,

'It's not my vision here. What do *you* think we should be doing to make this better?'"

At this point team managers often find something on the map that makes sense for their team to work on, and the team takes ownership of that piece. For example, one major hurdle that stood out on the credit-card acquisition maps was that customers needed to actually go to a bank branch to prove their identity. Working at the map, Westpac was able to create a mobile-phone-based proof of identity that allows customers to avoid a trip to a branch. This seemingly simple feature took a lot of work from multiple teams and departments at the bank.

Smith told us that it's not so much the customer journey maps, the design walls, or really any single road map artifact that creates value on its own. Rather, those artifacts serve as a backdrop for the most important part of the process: the collaborative gatherings at the design walls. By holding meetings and discussions at the walls, which are rich in research and in artifacts that the team has produced together, the wall gathering yields far greater value for all team members than the standard practice of making decisions in a meeting room after reviewing a presentation, or by debating decisions in a string of twenty emails over days. In this way, the design walls serve as the context in which teams can work together to align themselves around the same goals.

Addressing Experience Debt: Iteration Versus Increment

By building road maps around customer-centered journey maps, the Westpac team uses customer experience as a key dimension around which they align. This is a little bit different from the other examples we've shared in this chapter. Those teams used organizing principles that are more obviously based on business outcomes. There are advantages to organizing around customer experience, though, especially if it tracks to the strategic goal. At Westpac, this is indeed one of the strategic goals.

It can be hard to create a great customer experience in an agile context. One of the frustrations we see in some organizations that work in an agile way is something called experience debt, or design debt. Similar to *technical debt* (an engineering term for the engineering housekeeping-type work that is useful but never gets prioritized and thus builds up over time), *experience debt* comes from the small design problems that build up over time and reduce the quality of the user experience: a confusing instruction here, an extra pop-up window there.

Designers want to be able to go back and improve things by *iterating*: working on the feature again. But project owners, whose performance is sometimes measured by how many features they release, may feel pressure to move forward to the next feature. Muir points out that neither choice is inherently right or wrong. "It's a value trade-off," he told us. Muir says that the journey maps help make this choice visible. Teams can look at the map, see the work that remains to be done, see which customer pain point needs to be addressed (or even addressed again), and make choices in the context of the vision of the future.

Muir told us that the customer journey maps help address what he calls "the translation gap." This is the gap between what leaders want to do for customers and what they actually do. The gap isn't intentional, Muir says. "I've never talked to anyone in the organization who says, 'I want to give the customers a hard time.'" Instead, the gap comes from a lack of clarity and shared values. Stephen Bungay calls this phenomenon "the alignment gap," which he defines as "the difference between what we want people to do and what they actually do."[10] Muir notes that it helps when leadership is talking about being customer-centered, because people hear that message and can use it to guide their actions.

In other words, alignment starts with leaders who are clear about values, but creating alignment takes a lot of work. And it requires planning tools that can reinforce the values that leaders seek. This is why a good road map must create a link between the work that is being done by staff, the outcomes created by that work, and the way those outcomes will help the organization achieve its strategic goals.

Gaining the Value of the Human-Centered Perspective

Part of the power of the customer journey map is that it aligns the work of multiple teams around a single vision. It helps that it expresses the vision in terms of the customer, because this point of view cuts across the organization. It cuts across roles, departments, channels, and so on. It allows the organization to step outside itself and consider how the various pieces of the system fit together.

Leisa Reichelt, head of service design and user research at the Australian government's Digital Transformation Office, told us that in her work in government, it's common for this kind of user-centered planning to cut across many parts of the government. "When you have three levels of government [federal, state, and local] and many agencies, you can see programs that easily cut across twenty, thirty, or forty departments," she told us. The resulting coordination problem may seem overwhelming, but the potential to create valuable services makes this point of view important. It's the difference, she told us, between "giving someone a concession [health care discount] card when they turn sixty-five, versus helping someone transition to a new phase of life."

Planning Your Portfolio

The next level above program management is portfolio management. Large organizations must find ways to think about their investment across their entire product portfolio. How does the sense and respond approach apply in this context?

Let's start with an uncontroversial observation: there is no one-size-fits-all method for product success. Every project is different, every team is different, and an approach that works for one project is probably not appropriate for the next project. That said, there are patterns we can use to identify which projects benefit from which approaches, and we can use those patterns to identify the right approach.

Managing Uncertainty and the Product Life Cycle

As we've said, the major reason to adopt a sense and respond approach is to deal with uncertainty. When you think about the product portfolio, uncertainties tend to fall into three major categories:

- *Customer-related.* Is there a need? Does our solution satisfy the need?

- *Sustainability-related.* Is the business sustainable? Is the market large enough? Can we create technology and infrastructure and operations that allow us to deliver the service profitably?

- *Growth-related.* How can we grow the business?

Furthermore, these categories map more or less directly to the life cycle of a business. Some companies use this mapping explicitly. For example, at Intuit, a Silicon Valley-based maker of financial software and services, teams overlay these questions onto McKinsey &

Company's well-known three horizon model and use this model for portfolio management.

The *three horizon model* is a framework for managing growth. The model, formulated by Mehrdad Baghai, Stephen Coley, and David White in *The Alchemy of Growth,* asserts that growth should be understood in terms of three time horizons: near term, mid-term, and long term.[11] Horizon 1 is the near-term growth opportunity. Your core business lives here, and you should be managing it for growth and efficiency. Horizon 2 is where your emerging businesses live. These businesses must be nurtured. Some of them will become your core businesses in the midterm future. Finally, Horizon 3 is the long-term future. This is where new options are identified, evaluated, and either killed or promoted. The authors note that at any given time, your portfolio must contain projects in all three horizons.

At Intuit, teams map the three types of uncertainties onto the three horizon model.

- For horizon 3, they ask customer-related questions. Is there a need? Can we create a solution that satisfies the need? Will people buy our solution, and, most important, do people love it?

- For horizon 2, ideas that make it out of horizon 3 are evaluated in terms of their business viability: Can we make enough money on this to make it a worthwhile business? Can we make it efficient and repeatable? Can we find evidence that we can grow it large enough to make it worth our investment?

- For horizon 1—businesses that have customer love and are viable—the focus is on growth and efficiency. What can we do to make this business larger and more profitable?

Companies that are disciplined about product portfolio manage-ment recognize the value of balancing the portfolio in terms of risk, strategic fit, and stage in the product life cycle. Intuit balances its investment across the product life cycle by allocating budget across the three horizons, with 10 percent going to horizon 3, 30 percent going to horizon 2, and 60 percent going to horizon 1.[12]

Setting Financial Targets across the Portfolio

This final point from Intuit is critical to enabling good planning across the portfolio, because it points to the importance of managing your budget toward different goals and, by inference, with different yardsticks. About this process, former Intuit vice president Hugh Molotsi wrote, "A common mistake companies make is measuring the progress of all their offerings using standard business metrics—like revenue, profit and customer acquisition—no matter what stage those offerings are in. Horizon planning helps us avoid that mistake by providing guidance on what our expectations should be from of-ferings at each stage in their maturity."[13]

Intuit uses different targets for projects in each section of the portfolio. The current core businesses are measured much as we might expect, in terms of revenue, profitability, growth, and effi-ciency. For horizon 2, the emerging businesses, things are different. These business are trying to establish a foothold, so winning market share and demonstrating rapid growth rates matter more than prof-itability. Finally, for horizon 3 offerings, real financial results are set aside entirely. Those teams need to create a credible hypothesis about their business model, but they don't need to prove it. Instead, they are asked to prove what the company calls "customer love," meaning that they are looking for a problem and solution that the market wants.

Using Sense and Respond in Portfolio Management

All this serves as background to this question: How do we understand the sense and respond approach in the context of portfolio planning? The key is in understanding how you can apply sense and respond to each of the different types of uncertainties. Early-stage validation work, the horizon 3 work that seeks to identify customer love, is working at the largest scale of uncertainty. It is typical for almost every dimension of a business to be uncertain here: Who are the customers? What problem are they trying to solve? What solution can we create? How will we make money? This is classic startup territory.

In horizon 2, the level of resolution becomes one step finer. Presumably, you've found a business that works for a small set of customers. Here is where you're looking to prove you can be a profitable business, so your experiments are firmly about getting the business model right and moving toward profitability. But businesses in this stage of development are at their most vulnerable. They have left the protection of the R&D group or innovation lab, where many horizon 3 ideas are born and incubated. As organizational theorist and *Crossing the Chasm* author Geoffrey Moore says, these initiatives are "adolescents."[14] But too often they're held to the same operational metrics as the core businesses we find in horizon 1. This is a mistake, Moore argues. These businesses need to focus on finding their feet before they can deliver the profits we expect from our core businesses. The questions in this section tend to be about how you unlock growth, and the experiments should focus on the tactics you think will unlock growth. How can we get more customers for this business? What is stopping adoption? Are we serving the right use cases, or do we need to add or adjust? Are we serving the right market segment? Do we need to add adjacent segments?

Finally, in horizon 1, our core businesses, we can still use sense and respond tactics, but the resolution becomes finer still: it's about growing engagement and delivering and receiving more value from each customer. What features will we add? What costs can we cut without impacting quality?

Here's the bottom line: when you're figuring out how to assign work to teams and how to measure their performance, you have to remember that there is no single set of measures by which team performance can be assessed. Rather, leaders must consider where an initiative is in the life cycle and what uncertainties teams face. Only then can planners create appropriate missions for teams.

Sense and Respond Takeaways for Managers

✓ Changing the way you plan and assign work is one of the most important parts of a sense and respond approach.

✓ Leaders create the conditions in which sense and respond teams operate. Teams can try to "be agile" as much as they like, but if their direction is not constructed correctly—if their freedom to act isn't preserved, their goals are not defined correctly, and their constraints are not clearly understood—then there is little they will be able to do.

✓ Uncertainty changes the way you plan. Plans must be oriented toward the results teams are attempting to achieve.

✓ This new kind of planning has an impact at the team level; at the program level, where new methods of cross-team coordination must be employed; and at the portfolio level, where it is important to differentiate the different types of outcomes that teams seek across the product life cycle.

✓ Use the principle of mission command to direct teams. This means asking teams to achieve an outcome rather than to create a specific output.

✓ Coordinate the activity of multiple teams (programs) by using outcome-based road maps.

✓ Alignment around strategy becomes more important than ever and must be created by a robust communication process that combines top-down strategy, bottom-up insight, and two-way communication.

✓ In portfolio planning, you can use the idea of outcomes to create targets across the portfolio that are appropriate for different stages in the product life cycle.

6

Organize for Collaboration

At the heart of digital innovation is the small, cross-functional team. This team is the engine that powers modern software development, its smallest useful unit—the molecule. While industrial production is built around assembly lines, digital production is, increasingly, built around this small team.

Much has been written about how to make these teams work, and indeed these ideas have been widely adopted in Silicon Valley and other places where software is made. But it's worth spending a few moments here, before we go any further, to look at this small team and consider what makes it tick.

Hero Myths

There are two competing hero stories in the world of software. The first is of the lone hacker. We usually imagine this hacker as a twenty-something guy in a t-shirt, bleary eyes propped open with caffeinated beverages, clattering away on his keyboard in a dark room somewhere, wrestling all night with code and emerging in the light of day with a fantastic new creation. And even though these folks exist and some software development is done this way, we've learned that the lone hacker genius is better as a story than as a model to emulate and aspire to. Creativity appears in many forms and works in many styles, but lone creative geniuses capture our imagination precisely because they are rare and elusive.

The other story we hear is the startup in a garage. In this story, a small group of people—two, three, four, maybe five misfits—come together in pursuit of an idea. They bring different skills to the table—think Steve Jobs's vision and salesmanship combined with Steve Wozniak's engineering genius—and form a unit that is capable of launching the next billion-dollar company.

This second story is more realistic. It's a much closer match to what we know about how good software gets made. It gets made in small teams of people, aligned around a goal, bringing diverse skills to bear, and figuring it out as they go. Indeed, this story isn't so much an engineering story—although the engineering skill of these teams is understood to be a given. Rather, this story is a one of entrepreneurship. Of chasing a dream. Of making mistakes, learning, correcting, and finally breaking through.

The engine of digital production looks like the entrepreneurial team in the garage. At the heart of this team, you'll typically find a balanced group made up of all the diverse capabilities you need to launch a digital product or service and to quickly interpret the insight generated by the resulting two-way conversations. The people on these teams generally fill three core roles: engineering, product management, and design. These three capabilities form a three-legged stool. Engineering is concerned with what's feasible—what can be built. Product management is concerned with the viability of the business—how the business will sustain itself. Design is concerned with desirability—how you make something people want.[1]

Depending on the business context, you see a different balance of roles, and you often see additional roles. For example, a news site or content business will probably include editors and writers on the team. A retail business might include merchandisers. A business with a great deal of complexity might include business analysts or other specialists. But this cross-functional team is foundational. To get it to work, you need to set it up in the right way.

Transforming Digital Product Development

In 2012, PayPal, the electronic payments company, appointed David Marcus to the position of president. Marcus, who joined the company in 2011 when it acquired his startup, set out to transform PayPal from the slow, bureaucratic company it had become. His goal was to modernize the company and help it recapture the entrepreneurial spirit it once had. Marcus restructured the way people were assigned to teams. He limited the number of cross-office, cross-time-zone teams. He restructured the physical work spaces so that teams could sit together in collaborative work spaces. And he changed the way the product teams worked—moving them away from tightly specified, sequential "waterfall" approaches to a more agile approach.

One of the first projects PayPal took on using this approach was to reinvent PayPal's Checkout product. At the time Checkout generated 75 percent of PayPal's revenue, representing something like $3.5 billion of revenue. Marcus selected a small team, led by Bill Scott, a veteran technologist who had been recruited from Netflix, and set a goal to launch the redesigned experience in six weeks.

If this sounds aggressive to you, you're right, especially considering the situation at PayPal at the time. In 2011, it took on average 180 days to create an app—twenty-six weeks. Pushing through simple changes to a page could take six weeks. Changing text in the footer of a web page could take two months. Things were slow for two reasons. First, the company's technology platform had become fragmented over time, so implementing simple changes often required laborious and repetitive work. Second, the human processes—designing, approving, building, testing, and more approving—were slow and sequential. Work moved from one department to the next at a glacial pace.

The project to reinvent Checkout was called Hermes. Project Hermes gathered designers, product people, and developers in a room. They began a weekly cycle of designing, building, testing, and learning. They threw away their old sequential processes. Instead, designers and developers sketched together at a whiteboard and then went back to their desks and built what they had just sketched. They worked together to test what they had built with customers, observing what worked and what didn't and then revising their work based on what they learned. Informed by these two-way conversations with their target audience, they had a working app in days and, within weeks, one they were confident in. And even though they weren't able to ship in six weeks—the technology systems couldn't be changed as quickly as the human processes—they were able to start a significant transformation. The team members served as pioneers to help figure out how to change the things that PayPal needed to change to become more entrepreneurial.

If you fast forward to today, you'll see this new collaborative approach in use across PayPal. Projects are staffed with cross-functional teams. Those teams are able to push new code live in minutes instead of weeks. The company has made sweeping changes to work this way—changing not only the collaboration but also the technology stack, the office spaces, team assignments, and more.[2]

Enabling Experimentation and Learning through Collaboration

Why was this approach so important to PayPal, and why is it rapidly becoming the standard way that businesses integrate digital technology into their operations? It's because this type of collaboration allows teams to learn their way forward.

In the industrial model, we sequenced the flow of work through various stations and through various specialists. An automobile chassis passed through the assembly line, for example, and at each station, a specialist performed a set of operations on the chassis. In the digital age, as organizations scaled up, we often saw this approach replicated for digital product development.

At large digital agencies, for example, the production of websites for clients often moves through a predictable sequence of functional roles. Account people and technical salespeople scope and sell the work, determining in advance exactly what the scope of work will be. At the start of the project, strategists work to set the project strategy and refine the approach. Frequently, researchers come in next, working with customers or doing desk research. They package their insights into a report for the clients and also for the agency's design team. The researchers and strategists then move on to other projects, and the designers take over. Designers pick up the book of insights from researchers and proceed through *wire framing*—the process of creating the blueprint for the website—and then hand that work to another set of specialists to complete the graphic design. Once this is complete, the designs are passed down the line to the engineering staff, who build the thing. Finally, the work is passed to QA—quality assurance—whose specialists come up with a test plan and then test the site for bugs. After all this is done, the site is handed to an operations team, whose members are responsible for loading it onto a production server and launching the site. (Outsourced engineering firms frequently use some version of this process as well, although the early phases will be focused on requirements definition rather than strategy, and the design work is more likely technical design and creation of system architectures.)

The economics of the large agency seem to mandate this approach. In a large agency, staff utilization is the key metric, so agencies are structured to maximize the billable hours of every "resource." Thus, during a strategy definition phase, the strategists are working full time, but the rest of the specialists are idle. The client, understandably, doesn't want to pay for idle team members, so, unless the agency can find a way to get them billing, the agency has to pay people to be idle. As a result, these folks are typically assigned to other projects until their phase of work on the project can begin.

This is all perfectly sensible, and also completely wrong. Let's look at why.

Managing for Value Versus Utilization

The first problem here is that the original approach—the one conceived by the client and sales team—is likely to be only partially right. This means that it's also partially wrong. Projects need a way to correct for this situation, or else the early mistakes will be compounded. If decisions and information flow only one way—downstream—you never have the opportunity to correct mistakes as you go.

The second issue with this kind of project flow is that the knowledge you are creating in each phase of work gets lost at each hand-off point. Knowledge is not like a car chassis. It does not roll intact and complete down an assembly line. Instead, it grows and lives inside our heads. It is messy and can never be perfectly transmitted from one person to the next. No matter how well we document what we've learned, some of what we've learned stays in our head, and some of what we document gets misinterpreted or distorted by the biases of the transmitter or receiver.

This all adds up to a simple and overwhelming problem: the high likelihood of building the wrong thing. So the project approach is efficient but not effective. Utilization is high, but the output creates no value.

Creating the Self-Sufficient Team

The alternative to the industrial model is to create small, self-sufficient sense and respond teams. These teams are given autonomy to operate independently in pursuit of an assigned mission—to seek out and create value. An autonomous team has a full set of sense and respond capabilities and can create and participate in two-way conversations with the market.

Teams that are able to sense are allowed to interact with the market—to interact with and observe customers, to monitor how they're using the product, and to create probes, provocations, and tests in order to sense market needs with greater clarity. Teams that are able to respond are able to understand and interpret the sensing data, make decisions based on this data, and then produce a response.

So these are the capabilities of a sense and respond team: monitoring and observing customers, creating experiments, understanding and interpreting data, deciding how to respond, and producing a response.

These capabilities are not new, but the way we arrange them inside an organization is new. In industrial organizations, these capabilities are typically working in isolation and in sequence. In a sense and respond organization, there is no time for this work flow—and there is a distinct disadvantage created by the isolation this style of information flow creates.

Becoming a Self-Sufficient Team: Continuous Learning

Let's look at a story of two different teams at one company to see some of the factors that can make this approach successful or not.

In 2006, a team at a Wall Street brokerage was facing a challenge: the company was successful in its core electronic trading business, but executives knew that it needed to provide additional types of electronic trading services to diversify its offering.

The strategy and product management teams were divided on how to launch the new service. The managers all agreed that they needed to launch the service. They even agreed as to what type of trading service it needed to be. The disagreement was about how to deliver it to customers. In other words, the high-level strategy was clear and well supported. But there was little alignment about how to proceed.

In electronic trading, clients use a variety tools to send trades to their brokers. They can call or email or message them, they can send them through third-party trading applications, or they can send them through trading applications that the broker provides. The team at this brokerage was divided about which method it should choose.

Learning How to Proceed: Decisions and Alignment

There were three possible ways to deliver the new service to customers, and each idea had supporters.

1. Some members of the strategy team wanted to build a new "broker-neutral" app to give to customers. This new app would incorporate all of the trading services the company offered. It would also allow customers to trade with brokers at other competitive firms. Clients typically want to manage all their trades from one application regardless of which broker they're trading with, and this camp argued that customers wanted this functionality. Developing this system would be a big job.

2. Other managers argued the firm should build a similar app, but it should allow trading only with the firm: a "single-broker" app. People in this camp believed they shouldn't spend time helping customers trade with competitive brokers.

3. Finally, a third group argued that no app was needed at all. Instead, this group argued that the firm should simply make the service available to clients through clients' existing third-party trading apps.

The strategy and product management teams argued and pitched. Eventually, the executive team decided to build the single-broker app (option 2). It's important to note that this decision was made based on the strength of the argument and the persuasive ability of the advocates, rather than on market feedback.

Once this decision was made, the brief was given to the design team: create a single-broker app to deliver both the core business and the new business in one bundle.

The designers started their work by sending a team of designers and design researchers into the field to observe clients and interview them about their needs. They quickly found a problem. Clients wanted everything in one place. They were not likely to accept a big, new single-broker app.

The researchers went back to report their findings, but leadership was unwilling to revisit the decision. It had been a highly political and emotional process to get to the decision, and none of the parties were willing to spend political capital to revisit it. Instead, they directed the design team to stay on course. But the findings created doubt, and alignment started to suffer.

Using Incremental Versus Iterative Development

Next, a development team came onboard and got to work. Team members were worried about the ambitious technical challenges the project faced, and they conceived an incremental, agile approach to building the app. This approach involved breaking down the functionality into little pieces and building piece by piece. They estimated that it would take a little over a year before they would be ready to ship to customers.

Any observer who dropped in on the team at this point would have seen what looked like a remarkable collaboration. The team members did a great job of working together. Developers, designers, product managers, and QA testers all moved into a well-appointed "war room" and proceeded with great esprit de corps. Team members consulted each other about key decisions, used a lot of modern agile methods, and were dedicated to continuously improving their process.

The problem was this: the team never shipped the app to customers. Team members had set themselves such a large task—building an enormous application intended to replace competitors' existing mature offerings—that they couldn't get to the finish line. The iterative approach was good for technical problem solving—the team got key components working—but it never was able to create a solution that solved a user need from beginning to end.

With the seeds of doubt sown by the initial research starting to sprout, stakeholders became increasingly worried. Add to that the cost of delay: after two years, the team still hadn't delivered the service to customers. Stakeholders, understandably, ran out of patience, and the project was shut down. For most of that time, there were at least five to fifteen people working on the project. All of that effort, all of those hours—wasted.

Learning from the Abandoned Project

The following year, some of the folks from that team were assigned to a new project and vowed to correct their mistakes.

On this new project, the design team built a different kind of research phase. After an initial round of research that revealed learning that questioned the strategic plan, the design team took the strategy team on a weeklong road trip in order to do customer research together. The design team wanted to avoid the problem it faced previously, when it "reported" its findings. Instead, team members wanted decision makers to see with their own eyes.

This trip was a turning point in the new project. It allowed the strategy team to see what the design team was seeing. In fact, by experiencing it together, members of both teams learned more than they would have by either team doing the research alone. In addition, the experience created a collaborative relationship, rather than a political one, among the team members. This collaboration continued through the life of the project. In effect, it created one team.

When the team members returned from their road trip, they were determined to avoid another mistake of the earlier project effort: they were determined to ship as soon as possible. So although they had ambitious plans for the product they would eventually build, they asked themselves, "What's the smallest thing we can build in order to be in the market in three months or less?" They also added some additional collaborators to figure out the answer.

They pulled in the salespeople and traders who would be working on the service, and they pulled in the engineering team members who would be building it. This war room was very different from the earlier one. It's wasn't an engineering-only room or even a product-team-only room. It housed a self-sufficient business team. This team, working in a series of collaborative design sessions, sketched the outlines of a service that would be delivered, at least initially, mostly through human agents, backed up by a small amount of software. Over time, as they confirmed that the service was working as imagined, the team members planned to shift more of the functionality into the software in order to allow the service to scale.

And it worked. The team launched the service in a matter of months, to positive reaction in the market, and was able to scale it up through frequent follow-up releases in the subsequent year.

Capturing the Lessons

There are two important takeaways from this story. The first is about incremental development versus iterative development. The second is about team collaboration and alignment.

Incremental versus iterative

Incremental development starts with a grand vision: you look out into the future, plan something large, and set that large vision as your goal. You then decompose the vision into small pieces and build them incrementally. Think of building a house out of bricks. In software terms, this way of working has some advantages. By working in small units, you have the ability to build software that is technically robust; each unit can be tested and isolated, and you can build systems that are stable and easy to maintain and change over time.

The problem with incremental development is that, if you don't sequence the things you build correctly, you don't have anything that's "done" from a customer's point of view until the end; customers can't move into the house until the roof is on and all the windows are installed. This means that you don't start delivering value to the customer until the end of a very long process. Even worse, it means you don't start the two-way conversation to get customer feedback until the end. The first project at the brokerage used this approach, and because it never delivered value, it was vulnerable.

Iterative development is different. Because software is not the same as a brick building, it can shape-shift as you build it. So the plan might be to end up with a luxury hotel, but you might start by creating a tent and then adding a floor to turn it into a luxury tent; then you might add walls to make it a cabin, then a roof, and so on. So you're providing value to a customer from the earliest stages and delivering an increasingly valuable solution with each iteration you release to the market. And with each of these iterations you're getting feedback from your customers as the system evolves. The second project at the brokerage used this approach and was able to deliver value to customers early, helping ensure project success.

Team collaboration

Team collaboration is what makes iterative development possible. Iterative approaches require a humble mindset regarding the vision you've laid out. You still have a vision—that's critical—but you have to be willing to admit that you're not certain your plan will work. When you do this, you can then position your team to receive feedback and make decisions in response to that feedback. For this to work, you have to acknowledge that those decisions will not be made once, but rather will be made continuously, in response to each iteration.

The first step in creating a team capable of responding to what it learns is to create a self-sufficient, cross-functional team. On software teams, this means design, engineering, and business experts are working together in a tight collaborative loop. It's important that this collaborative team not be simply a collection of technical specialists; that kind of collaboration is important, but, as you saw in the earlier story, it's not enough. If the team is really working to deliver value to the customer and the business, then the business decision makers need to be part of the collaborative loop.

Including business decision makers has a second impact. It creates an alignment between the team that's doing the work and the people who are deciding what work to do, both inside and beyond team boundaries. As you saw in this story, it's one thing to make a decision—but a very different thing to create alignment around that decision.

Gaining the Power of Cross-Functional Teams

It's not just digital teams that are discovering the power of cross-functional organization.

In January 2013, Chip Blankenship, then CEO of GE Appliances, put a small, cross-functional team in a room and challenged it to deliver a new, high-end French-door refrigerator to production in twelve months, or about a quarter of the time it normally takes to create a new refrigerator.[3] As if this weren't enough, he wanted a working product in three months. Blankenship had embraced the lean startup movement and wanted to see whether he could apply it to appliance development.

The only way that the team could move this quickly was to bring everyone together and dedicate them to this one task.

As team members began to think through how they were going to make their deadline, they identified the constraints in their traditional process. They realized that to move at a faster pace they would need to build a continuous flow of insight from salespeople, designers, material suppliers, and customers. In the traditional model it could take months to work through conversations with all of these stakeholders and participants. The team wanted to bring that down from months to days, or even hours. Team members knew they'd have to shorten those time lines if they were going to hit their deadlines. And it wasn't just discussions that would have to move more quickly. The team wanted to generate fast market feedback, so it would need a way to involve customers. Finally, the team knew it would also have to be able to respond quickly with design updates as it learned what worked: it needed everyone involved in the process to be aware of the new pace at which the team expected to move.

The team had early discussions with suppliers, who were thrilled to be a part of the process: it gave the suppliers a preview of the product to come and the new ability to plan which materials they'd need to produce to support manufacturing at scale.

The team included a finance person, too: it realized that its traditional business case calculations wouldn't work on this project. Normally, with multiyear project time frames, finance is far removed from the product team. There just isn't much that changes day-to-day from a finance perspective on a typical appliance project. This project was different. The team needed a finance person who understood what the team was trying to do and could help it create a new model for this new approach. It needed to create a business case that was flexible enough to respond to the frequent adjustments it was making.

Finally, leadership realized that top-down decision making wasn't going to work if this team was going create a great product in twelve months. There simply wasn't enough time for each decision to be run up the chain for the traditional set of approvals and sign-offs. The team would need more decision-making authority than normal. By embedding decision-making autonomy in the team, leadership enabled team members to move quickly enough to make several iterations over the course of the year.

The end results speak for themselves. The product is selling at twice the normal rate, costs half as much, and got to market twice as fast as previous refrigerators.

Although the refrigerator itself is not a software-driven product, the techniques and attitudes used in pulling together the team, creating its mission, and empowering it to pursue that mission are techniques that work in any domain in which teams face uncertainty.

Managing Teams with the Orbital Model

In this core team model, we've said there are people in three major functional areas who must collaborate: design, technology, and business. Beyond that, though, teams will often have other core contributors, frequently dedicated business or domain specialists. Taproot Foundation, introduced in chapter 5, operates an online job-matching service that brings employers and specialist employees together to work on projects. The team that manages the online marketplace includes community managers. Running the service successfully requires deep, continuous contact with the communities that participate in the service, so simply running a website with one team and delivering the service with another team doesn't make sense. These capabilities work together on a daily basis.

Other companies may have a business need to maintain separate teams but work to create close collaborative relationships among them. In journalism, for example, the desire to protect editorial content from being influenced by business concerns led to the creation of the so-called Chinese wall that companies maintain between those departments. But these walls are becoming increasingly problematic. In fact, the *New York Times Innovation Report,* described in chapter 4, explicitly called for better collaboration across this wall. The authors wrote, "There are a number of departments and units, most of which are considered part of the business side, that are explicitly focused on the reader experience, including Design, Technology, Consumer Insight Group, R&D and Product. These functions represent a clear opportunity for better integration."[4]

At digital-native media firms, we're starting to see this wall crumbling. Emerging news organizations make fewer distinctions between editorial and product. At BuzzFeed, for example, one engineer describes the collaboration this way: "Being able to work closely with our Editorial Team and Business Department is one of the most rewarding parts of my job. I build technology for people who work across the room from me."[5] At Vox Media, the collaboration rules are built into the company code of conduct:

> Editorial team members and others across the company
> are our peers and collaborators, not our clients. We main-
> tain open lines of communication and foster good working
> relationships—indeed, friendships—with our colleagues.
> And we often switch roles: Product members write for
> our editorial teams; writers and editors serve as product

managers, designers, and engineers; and advertising staff-ers contribute to the same products that we all use. That collaboration is core to our success.[6]

Many teams require specialists if they are to succeed, although they don't require these specialists on a daily basis. You might need someone from your company's legal or compliance team available to review work, but you probably don't need them daily. The same might be true for any range of specialists.

For this, we're seeing teams use what we call the *orbital model* of staffing. In this model, your core team is a planet, and you have a variety of specialists orbiting the planet like moons. This model works because, like a moon, each specialist is on a known orbit. Specialists check in with the team once or twice a week—an agreed-upon cadence. It's the rhythm of this relationship that makes it work. Unlike other part-time staffing assignments, in the orbital model, the key to making the assignment work is the known and consistent rhythm of the interaction.

There are solid economic models that process specialists use to determine whether a given specialist belongs on a core team or whether that specialist should contribute to many teams on a part-time basis. A common example is the idea of a fire department; should every company have a firefighting squad? For most businesses, the answer is no: it makes sense to rely on centrally provided city services. There will be some businesses, though—perhaps those that burn things as a core operation—that need firefighting on site.

Another benefit of the orbital model is the perception of the people who are in orbit. In many cases we've observed that these folks are perceived as obstacles to getting work done: "We'd love to launch this faster, but the brand and risk people have to review everything we do." By including these noncore disciplines in the conversation on a regular basis, the organization ensures that they are perceived as members of the team. Regular interactions break down perceptions that these disciplines are there to "get in the way." This rhythm smooths relationships and reduces the friction in getting products to market faster.

This points to the important social component of a good team. When you walk into a team space for a good team, you can feel it. People like each other. They tell jokes. They trust each other. They know whom to talk to for a given concern, and they are proactive in addressing these concerns. The orbital model, which makes for a standing connection between core and noncore team members, creates a kind of ongoing, committed relationship that helps these social ties grow.

Making Collaboration Possible

Managers can create the conditions for collaboration to flourish by making a few changes in the way teams are composed, managed, and organized. These changes are simple enough to describe but can be difficult to implement, because they require coordination with other departments. Indeed, without the support of senior leadership, these changes may prove quite difficult to achieve, as simple as they may seem.

Here is a list of key changes that enable sense and respond teams to collaborate effectively:

- Creating autonomous, mission-based teams

- Using cross-functional teams

- Building dedicated teams

- Supporting new work flows

- Co-locating teams

- Being careful with remote work

- Being careful with outsourcing

- Holding retrospectives and using minimum viable processes

Think of this list as a starting point rather than a recipe. Every organization that implements these ideas will need to do so in a slightly different way. Think of these points as principles rather than hard-and-fast rules.

Creating Autonomous Teams with Outcome-Based Missions

Earlier, we covered the concept of outputs versus outcomes. The idea is that teams should not be ordered to create a specific output but instead should be asked to achieve a certain outcome—for example, "Figure out how to launch our new trading service." To achieve their mission, then, teams need to decide what to make and need to have the resources they need to make it, the ability to release it, and the permission to learn and begin again. This means that the team must have capabilities that cover the spectrum of these activities. They also need the authority to execute these activities without waiting for approval. They need freedom of action.

With these capabilities, they are able to move quickly and learn their way forward.

Without these capabilities, however, bad things happen: when teams wait for approval, they become dependent on outside decision makers. They slow down. They can't respond when the moment is appropriate. They limit their techniques. They limit their ability to learn. They limit their ability to deliver value.

So, when facing uncertainty, autonomous teams that are capable of learning are the ones that will create value for your organization.

Creating Cross-Functional Teams

Earlier in this chapter, we describe the capabilities of autonomous teams: monitoring and observing customers, creating experiments, understanding and interpreting data, deciding how to respond, and producing a response. These capabilities form the heart of the cross-functional teams we seek to create. In practice, this means we must build teams from cross-functional groups and make sure that the core team functions—design, engineering, and product management—are dedicated to that team.

One obstacle here is the shortage of skilled staff. Technology workers are in short supply, and it's often difficult to hire and retain enough people to get the work done. Compounding this problem is a legacy of understaffing designers in organizations. Designers, once considered a luxury in the software world, are now a necessity for most teams. But organizations are struggling to adjust their staffing levels. In older organizations we often see ratios of one designer to every one hundred technology staffers. As a result, these folks are spread thin, and they typically work in central service departments that function as internal agencies. We believe that a more effective ratio is one designer for every ten engineers and, for some organizations, even higher. Some teams can get away without designers, especially those working on back-end and middleware functionality, but any team with customer- or user-facing functionality should not forgo design.

Another common obstacle is the lack of coordination across functional departments. For many organizations, functional departments are allocated budgets without consideration of or coordination with other departments. So even though it may be in a team's interest to have fully cross-functional staffing, the department into which a given person reports may not share those interests. Solving this problem means that cross-department planning during the budgeting process is critical.

Creating Dedicated Teams

Once you have cross-functional teams, you need to ensure they are dedicated to a single mission at a time and that the staff is dedicated to the team.

Again, this may not be as simple as it sounds. It can be vexingly difficult. Often, there is more work to do than staff to do it. As a result, organizations try to squeeze more work out of each staff member by assigning the staffer to multiple projects. In a physical factory, the absurdity of this way of assigning work is obvious. You can't have someone working at two manufacturing stations simultaneously. But with thought work, the work itself is so abstract that it can shape-shift when assignments are being considered.

The problem with assigning staff to multiple teams or multiple projects is that it creates dependencies among projects, and dependencies reduce flow. Although a single team can schedule tasks together and optimize its flow internally, it becomes much harder for two teams to schedule tasks together. If a designer has to produce a drawing for team A, then her work for team B is idled until that drawing is complete. And if two people on team A have responsibilities to other teams—for example, the designer owes work to team A and the developer owes work to team C—then the scheduling problem suddenly multiplies in complexity and rapidly becomes unmanageable.

It is far better to keep things simple and efficient by dedicating staff to a single team and dedicating that team to a single mission.

Changing Work Flows

Perhaps the most important change you need to make in terms of collaboration is helping the team itself to reimagine its work flow. This kind of collaboration typically requires team members to change the way they accomplish their individual work. Product managers may be accustomed to creating detailed plans and business cases; they need to change their approach to one of asking questions and running experiments. Designers may be good at working out each pixel in Photoshop; they need to become comfortable facilitating team design sessions at the whiteboard. Developers may be used to working from detailed requirements documents; they must get used to starting with much sketchier inputs. And everyone needs to get used to the idea that change and rework are valuable parts of the process, instead of costs to be avoided.

According to PayPal's Bill Scott, reflecting on one reason his teams at his former employer, Netflix, were so successful, "I realized that, especially in the UI layer, we were throwing out 90 percent of the code we wrote in a given year."[7] The team there bought into the idea of continuous improvement: it's not that team members were writing bad code but that they thought of the code they were writing as simply a learning tool. It was part of the team's ongoing effort to find the right solution.

Creating Co-Located Teams

Once you have a single team and have dedicated it to a single project, you have the conditions for creating good collaboration. At least, you have the foundation upon which you can build. The next step is to get the team members working together.

The easiest way to get people working together is to put them in the same room. People who sit together will more naturally use conversation as a communication tool. It seems perhaps overly simple to say this, but in an age of text messaging, chat rooms, email, and videoconference, the power of face-to-face conversation is still hard to overstate.

A few years ago, we had the experience of working with a team of folks who had spent a year together working on a project in a single, open work space. These were people from different departments and specialties who had to learn to work together. Over the year, they became good collaborators, and they also became friends. But as the project was winding down, the members moved out of their shared space and back into their departmental spaces on opposite sides of the building. Another project team needed the room, so the team agreed to move. Still, there were a few loose ends to tie up, so the team members kept working, but now they weren't sitting together.

On the day after the team moved, a simple question from a QA tester on the team exploded into a conflict. The tester asked a fellow tester how a feature she was working on should work. The second tester didn't know and suggested calling the designers on the other side of the building. If the designers had been in the room, one of them would have heard the question and answered it, and the team would have moved on. Instead, the tester, perhaps not sure which designer to ask, wrote a note to the QA manager. The QA manager wrote a note to the design manager. The design manager asked the designer. The designer got annoyed. He thought that the tester had gone over his head to question his work to his manager. The designer wrote a snippy note back to the tester, who forwarded the note to her manager, and eventually the team needed to call a mediation session in a conference room to deal with the email chain. Never mind that the original question was simple, even trivial. And never mind that only two days before, the tester would have simply looked up and asked the designer a question, and they both would have moved on.

This isn't to say that being in the same room is the only way to create good collaboration or that simply putting people in the same room automatically creates collaboration. But it gives it an important head start.

Managing Remote Collaboration

Perhaps no topic in technology teams is more hotly debated than that of remote work. Remote teams and remote work have long been part of the tech world. In fact, thought work is uniquely suited to remote work. Computers and the internet have given us the tools to work from anywhere, and many workers cherish this freedom.

Creating good collaboration with remote workers is harder than with co-located workers, though, and it requires much more conscious effort. This is because often, some team members are remote and others are co-located. When this happens, it creates imbalanced information flows that can reduce the effectiveness of remote workers. When some workers are hanging around the water cooler chatting and exchanging casual information, whether or not it is related to the project, it creates a communication channel that the remote worker cannot access. This is when things get out of balance.

When you're planning teams with remote workers, it is important to pay particular attention to things that create unbalanced communication, or things that interrupt real-time communication. Teams should generally be structured across as few time zones as possible so that people are awake at the same time. And to build the social relationships and trust that make collaboration possible, teams should plan to get together in person on a regular basis every few months at minimum.

Managing Outsourcing and Offshore Teams

Starting at the end of the 1980s and continuing through the 1990s and 2000s, we saw a rise in the use of outsourced and offshore IT services. Outsourcing companies offered a seemingly attractive proposition: by making use of low-cost IT and software engineering services, companies could avoid managing these nonstrategic business functions themselves, outsource them to high-quality experts, and free the client companies to focus on their core competencies.

As we hope we've made abundantly clear by now, IT and software development must now be considered a core strategic business function and must become a core competency for every firm of any size. For projects and programs in which uncertainty plays a significant factor, companies are increasingly moving away from IT outsourcing. Recently, we've seen an increasing trend to bring IT services in-house.[8]

Outsourcing is often associated with *offshoring,* the practice of moving work to other parts of the world to achieve efficiencies in hiring, diversity, cost, and schedule. Offshoring can happen with vendors, but it can happen within companies as well. Many companies locate business, sales, and marketing at headquarters in a major city and create engineering centers located many thousands of miles away. Outsourcing and offshoring create similar challenges. Both tactics create teams of workers who are separated from customers and stakeholders and are not capable of autonomous learning, and who face obstacles in building good collaboration with their colleagues in the business and who cannot, by themselves, establish a two-way conversation with the market.

There are, of course, technology projects that are suited to outsourcing. Not every technology project faces the same level of uncertainty. Projects with low uncertainty (about what to build and what will work) are candidates for outsourced or offshore teams. One way we've seen this work is with so-called two-track agile approaches.

In *two-track agile,* two tracks of work act in coordination. The first track is the experiment track. This team uses all the sense and respond techniques described in this book to take on the high-uncertainty portions of the work and figure out what solution works best. From there, the solution can be passed off to a second track—the production track—and this team implements the solution in a robust way. This arrangement works best when the hand-off between the teams is not a document, specification, or contract, but rather a working prototype that has been produced in the final delivery technology.

Two-track agile has the benefit of allowing one team to move quickly to discover market needs, and another team to work at a more measured pace to handle security, internationalization, scale, and other concerns. But doing it well is tricky. It risks generating some of the old problems we face with assembly line work: that information may not flow back to the product team in a timely fashion and that it will reduce the rate of change that's possible. It also isolates the production track, costing it the opportunity to get a preview of (or the ability to participate in defining) what's coming in the future.

Therefore, it's critical to establish some parameters if you're adopting two-track agile. It must allow fast feedback from production systems to the experiment track and must allow the *entire* system to iterate quickly in response to feedback. If members of the production track believe their responsibility is to implement features once and only once, the system will not work. Finally, it needs a way to create transparency between the two tracks of work so that some collaboration can happen even across tracks.

Holding Retrospectives

One of the most valuable techniques for improving team process is the *retrospective meeting,* in which periodically—usually every two or three weeks—the team members get together to discuss and improve their working process. There are many ways to run these meetings, but the point is to apply the sense and respond mindset to the team itself. What is working? What isn't working? What can we change in order to make things better?

In other words, the team members consider their process, like their product efforts, as a candidate for continuous improvement. We often advise teams to start with a minimum viable process and use retrospectives and continuous feedback (from inside and outside the team), along with process experimentation, to improve how they're working and collaborating.

In the beginning, these retrospective meetings may be painful. If teams aren't used to these discussions, or if they've been working together for a long time without them, then the first open discussion of problems can feel uncomfortable. But in the same way that products don't get better without feedback, your process must be examined in order to be improved.

One of the famous tactics of the Toyota production system is that anyone who observes a production problem has the power to stop the production line. This approach prevents the production of defects and allows the factory to detect and correct problems quickly.

In a similar way, frequent retrospectives focus the team on the quality of its "manufacturing" process and allow it to rapidly inspect and adapt in order to improve its work.

Sense and Respond Takeaways for Managers

✓ Small, self-sufficient, cross-functional teams are the key working unit of the sense and respond approach. These teams have the ability to monitor and observe customers, create experiments, understand and interpret data, decide how to respond, and produce a response.

✓ The core functions of the collaborative team tend to include design, engineering, and product management but frequently have other roles, depending on the organization.

✓ To create this collaboration, consider using autonomous, mission-based teams, cross-functional teams, and dedicated teams.

✓ Support new work flows, and create co-located teams. If you use remote or outsourced workers, be careful to assess their effect on the agile process.

✓ Adopting a minimum viable process and holding regular retrospectives will help team members collaborate more effectively.

7

Continuous Everything

Do Less, More Often

AutoTrader UK is the largest motor-vehicle classified advertising site in the United Kingdom. Founded in 1977 as a print publication, it launched its first website in 1996. In 2013, it made a complete transition to digital when, in June, it shut down its print business for good. AutoTrader UK now controls more than 80 percent of the market share there, according to the company.[1]

Before the company's transition to a digital-only business, the product team released website updates once or twice per year. When digital service became the team's only focus, it doubled that pace to quarterly releases. As you would expect, each time the team released new product features, customers responded with feedback. And not all of it was positive.

It would have been easy for managers to be discouraged by negative feedback, or to write it off because it contradicted their worldview. Instead, they embraced the feedback as an opportunity to learn. They thought, "If each time we roll out new software, we learn where we were right and where we wrong, then the more frequently we ship new ideas, the faster we'll be able to learn and adjust." They started asking themselves, "Why do we learn only four times a year? Why not four times a week?"

This idea—that you can increase the rate at which your organization learns by increasing the flow of ideas through the product development process—is fundamental to successful sense and respond approaches.

People who study processes are fascinated by the idea of flow—how you create it, how you maintain it, and how you gain the economic benefits of promoting it. For our purposes, the key insight is that the efficient flow of work through your organization and to the market, if done correctly, will create many benefits. AutoTrader UK wanted to increase the flow of learning by getting faster feedback from the market. In other words, it wanted to build and maintain a continuous two-way conversation with its market.

There's another benefit to shipping more frequently: a reduction in the *cost of delay*: if a feature is going to provide value, then you will reap more value by having it in the market sooner. Conversely, the longer you wait to ship, the less value you are able to capture. This value that you lose by not shipping is the cost of delay.

So there are solid economic reasons to optimize your organization to deliver new ideas to the market. This includes ideas embodied in software (such as a new feature on a website) as well as ideas that have nothing to do with software, such as pricing changes or new marketing messages. In modern businesses, many of these ideas rely on software for implementation, but all of this, as you will explore in this chapter, goes well beyond simply optimizing the software team. We have to look beyond the borders of the technology teams and consider the whole organizational system if we hope to create efficient flow.

Looking at the Infrastructure of Flow

To get started, let's talk about some of the technology practices that modern teams put in place to create the infrastructure for flow. Then we'll build on that to see how business teams are operating in this new environment of "continuous everything."

Assessing the DevOps Movement: The Technical Foundation of Flow

One of the most exciting things to emerge from the technology world in the past decade is the DevOps movement. DevOps—the word comes from combining *development* with *operations*—is a set of ideas and processes that make it possible for teams to release software frequently, reliably, and with less risk than before. DevOps is the technical and infrastructure foundation layer of what we've been talking about throughout this book, so it's worth spending a few minutes on the basic concepts that go into it and the impact it has on organizations.

To most people outside the technology industry, "software operations" are an invisible and obscure function. But operations are the folks who create and maintain the operating environment in which software products and services run. They set up servers and networks and databases, install and maintain the software that keeps all that infrastructure running well, deal with outages, and—most critically for this discussion—deploy the new versions of the software that product development teams create.

As we've discussed previously, in the early days of software development, software was created and delivered in a sequential process that resembled an assembly line. One set of people specified the software, another set designed it, another built it, another group tested it, and finally, the operations people deployed it. But as the developers at the heart of the process moved to agile methods and began releasing smaller and smaller chunks of code, the processes surrounding software development came under pressure.

Imagine you're a quality assurance tester. You're used to getting a big new chunk of software every month or so. That means you have plenty of testing time before the next batch arrives. Now imagine the pressure you face when developers start giving you software every two weeks, or every day, or even multiple times a day. The only way to keep up is to change your process, change your work flow, change your tools. You incorporate earlier collaboration, new testing strategies, and automated tests. This isn't about working harder or faster. It's about using automation. It's about fundamentally restructuring the work of the QA function.

The same thing has happened with operations work flows. With less-frequent software releases, teams could get away with slow, manual processes. Deploying new software could be scheduled for a Friday night to avoid any risk to systems used during business hours. Never mind that these Friday night deployments could last all weekend; as long as they got done by Monday morning, it was fast enough.

As releases become more frequent, though, the deployment operations could no longer keep pace. Operations teams also began to automate their processes, change their work flow, and increase collaboration with developers. These new approaches are what we refer to when we talk about DevOps, and they have enabled phenomenal changes. While companies were once excited to release new software a few times a year, we're routinely seeing companies that have taken up DevOps approaches releasing new software multiple times a day.

Understanding That Flow Is Not (Just) a Technical Problem

The team at AutoTrader UK knew all about DevOps. Leadership at the company included CEO Trevor Mather, whose previous role had been running one of the leading agile engineering consulting firms in the world, so he and his leadership team were well acquainted with the DevOps movement.

AutoTrader technology director CTO Chris Kelly told us, "[Our goal] is to provide a platform which encourages continuous delivery of features by product squads, and to provide the tools and frameworks to allow teams to measure and monitor their applications running in production."[2] In other words, AutoTrader UK wants to empower its teams to get their ideas out into customers' hands as quickly as possible and then monitor the performance of those features to understand whether they've been successful.

As the organization developed its technical capability to release software more frequently, though, other issues became apparent. The company was, in the words of COO Nathan Coe, "digital by revenue, not by nature." Indeed, for thirty-six years the organization had functioned as a print publisher. Consequently, that was its culture. The team structures, incentives, and day-to-day work flows had their roots in a print-based business. Executives realized, Cole said, that the company needed "a cultural change first. Then a business a change, and lastly, a technological one."

Managing Continuous Everything

In chapter 6 we talk about the importance of small, cross-functional, self-sufficient teams. But in an organization of any size, no team is truly self-sufficient. Teams rely on leadership to create their missions, provide funding, and establish boundaries within which they can operate. They rely on marketing and sales for certain kinds of interactions with the market. In short, there are many points of coordination, and not all of them can be swept away by bringing those functions into the team itself. So even though "self-sufficient" is a useful guideline for teams, truly 100 percent self-sufficient teams will rarely exist, and even more rarely will they make economic sense.

Instead, organizations must operate in a coordinated way. In the past, in manufacturing organizations, we often had at the core of the business a predictable, repeatable process, and we could create coordination because the business had predictable rhythms and time lines. The annual budget. The model year. The monthly sales plan. The weekly magazine. The daily newspaper. This made command and control models of management plausible. The central organization could understand and predict the operating rhythms of the business. In sense and respond organizations, coordination is more organic, and it happens, when it happens, by means of alignment and through mission command, both of which we discuss in chapter 5.

All this comes down to one simple idea: as we move from manufacturing of discrete items to a world of continuous production—as embodied by DevOps—it is important to consider our other discrete processes and transition them to continuous ones that can match the rhythm and pace of our new ways of creating products and services.

Controlling the Customer Experience: Look and Feel

One common fear that managers have about the move to continuous production has to do with the customer experience. Managers worry that continuous change will be disruptive or even, in some cases, dangerous to customers who rely on their products. How do you gain the benefits of flow without creating a chaotic, ever-changing experience for customers?

One popular technique that we've seen emerge is called the design system, or live style guide. Most large companies have a book of *brand standards* that define how everything should look and feel, from the company colors and logo standards to the way furniture is laid out in retail stores. These days, these brand standards are being supplemented by *design systems,* which live on the web and contain the parts that designers and developers can use to create the customer-facing elements of digital products. These systems are more than reference works; they are actually asset libraries. In other words, designers and developers can go to these sites and get the code they need for their project. When done well, design systems have proven very popular with product teams and those responsible for the customer experience.

Companies like GE and Westpac have public-facing design systems that allow product teams to move forward quickly without rewriting front-end code and without getting caught up in small conversations about things like button color. These design systems are essentially complete platforms that have been created to remove the repetitive conversations and tasks from the day-to-day work of the execution teams. Using these platforms, teams can use preapproved elements: they no longer have to make (or debate) minor decisions about the way the product looks. This allows teams to focus on the innovative, unique, and challenging needs of the system, and to move at a pace that creates a responsive conversation with the market. One manager told us that a design system "is what allows us to move forward so quickly. We never get bogged down talking about stuff that's already been decided."

Controlling the Customer Experience:
Features and Experiments

Beyond making sure that the software they ship looks good and reflects organization standards, managers need a way to control the features delivered to the market. After all, just because you can deliver software to the market multiple times a day doesn't mean that you want to do that. Instead, managers need to roll out new ideas in a way that serves their goals and the goals of the customer.

Most organizations that implement DevOps approaches have a way for managers to control which end users see which new features and when. This control is provided by something called *feature flags*, or *feature toggles*. You can think of these as on-off switches for features. They allow product managers to do things like experiment with new features by exposing them to only a small, selected group of users. Feature flags make it possible to A/B test alternative versions of a feature and to kill features that are causing confusion. And generally, they ensure that the decision to deploy software is a business decision rather than a technical decision.

The good news is that this capability gives managers tremendous new power. It gives organizations much more granular control over what the customer sees and when. Thus, the entire life cycle of a feature can be placed under the control of the team that has developed it. On the other hand, sometimes there are good organizational reasons to coordinate feature releases. For example, many online retail businesses limit changes to their website during the holiday shopping season. This is the major earning window for retail business, and caution is warranted at this point. Other businesses may have customers who are change averse; a merchant who uses an online service to do payroll every month doesn't want to have to learn new features every month. And, of course, some situations have safety implications, and vendors of such systems need to maintain appropriate controls.

Still, many of the formal release-management controls that were put in place in an earlier technological era are out of date. The US government, for example, put in place mandates in 2002 that guide procedures for releasing new software. Among other things, they stipulate that all government agencies conduct a privacy impact assessment (PIA) for any update to a system that collects personally identifying information. It's a well-intentioned idea, but when a PIA takes three weeks, that causes significant problems for an agile team hoping to release software every day. US government software teams are grappling with this problem as we write.

There's no blanket solution here except to recognize the principle that authority to release should be pushed down as low as possible— to the team level, in most cases—and that clear limits on authority and action should be established so that teams know when they need to coordinate with others to make release decisions.

Creating the Sandbox: A Safe Place to Play

Let's go back to the idea of mission command for a moment. Good orders in a mission command communicate to subordinates a mission to be completed in terms of the desired result. They don't specify how the subordinates should accomplish the mission. The choice of tactics is, within specified constraints, largely left to the people receiving the order. This last part is important. People in a mission command system are given freedom to act, but that freedom is not absolute. Freedom to act exists within clearly defined constraints.

We can bring this idea back to organizational work with the idea of a *sandbox*: a safe place with clear borders within which teams may operate. A sandbox creates positive effects for leaders as well as subordinates. For leaders, there is a legitimate fear that their people will get creative in some way that will cause trouble, and for which a leader will be held responsible. Creating clear guidelines within which people can operate can ease this fear. For subordinates, the fear is about crossing some unstated line. If leaders make the lines clear, it creates space for creativity.

Here's an example: at one large firm we spoke to, managers were free to put up experimental websites without asking permission, but they couldn't mention the company's name or use the brand elements anywhere on these pages. These teams were also not permitted to collect any personally identifiable information, or PII, without going through a review of their plans with a security team.

At another firm we spoke to, a consumer business with millions of customers, teams were free to reach out to customers to try out experimental services, as long as no experiment reached out to more than one hundred customers at a time. Teams that wanted to reach out to more customers had to get approval for their plans. At this organization, there was no prohibition against collecting PII, as long as it was handled within company guidelines. There was a restriction on collecting payments.

As with many things in the sense and response world, the boundaries that a sandbox articulates can be hard to anticipate. More often, teams stumble across a prohibition and have to figure out how to deal with it. For example, a team might request access to a company's mailing list, only to face scrutiny about their plans. This moment of scrutiny is the moment to start building the sandbox. Teams need to explain their motivation—for example, "We want to test this idea"—and work with the internal stakeholders to establish a guideline that everyone can live with. In general, stakeholders should be engaged early to establish standing rules by which to operate, rather than engaged in a one-off manner each time the issue is raised. When teams take this approach, proactively establishing new operating rules that form a sandbox, it can go a long way toward making everyone involved more comfortable with the new pace of operations, experimentation, and change that is now available to teams.

Finally, it's worth noting that sandboxes and explicit constraints are not necessarily the only way to give teams the freedom to operate. We talk about culture in more detail in chapter 8, but for now, note that over time, many organizations find that as they adopt this approach, they learn to trust that people will do the right thing. Indeed, AutoTrader UK is now nearing twenty-five hundred releases annually, and COO Coe notes key transformations in the way the company operates, including a move away from a formal process toward greater team autonomy and empowerment and a shift toward greater product ownership and common sense.

Managing beyond Budgeting: Even Planning Is Continuous

In this world of continuous, rapid change, some things stick to slower rhythms. Perhaps nowhere is this more true than in our financial processes, which are dominated by the annual budgeting process. If you've worked as a manager in an organization of any size, you've no doubt taken part in the budgeting process, a process that takes so long and consumes so much energy and attention that we often refer to October through December as *budgeting season*. How terrible that a process that adds so little value requires an entire season to complete! Even worse, by calling it a "season" we seem to grant it the inevitability of nature. "Sure, it's snowing now," we say with a shrug. "It's winter."

Why would organizations want to reconsider the budgeting process? If it's possible to learn continuously, why would you limit your power to respond by making annual plans that resist change?

We all know the problem of "use it or lose it" budgets. In this situation, you create a plan for a project, manage to get it funded and thus written into the budget for the forthcoming year, and then you embark on the project. In a sense and respond world, you may discover that your plan was based on some seriously flawed assumptions. What do you do? The right thing to do might be to abandon the effort entirely, but then what happens to the money? *Use it or lose it.* After spending an entire season fighting for the money, managers are understandably reluctant to surrender it.

Indeed, the Beyond Budgeting Institute, an international working group dedicated to changing corporate management models, argues that the annual budgeting cycle is deeply flawed. The number one problem it cites? "Budgeting prevents rapid response. [Businesses] need to respond rapidly to unpredictable events but the annual budgeting process was never designed for this purpose."[3]

Sonja Kresojevic, senior vice president of global product lifecycle at Pearson, the global educational publishing company, told us, "You need to become a responsive organization." She went on, "Twenty years ago, Pearson was a print publishing business. It was a very predictable business. Now, as we move into digital, success and failure is more volatile and we need to adapt our process to respond to that change."[4]

To become more responsive, Pearson is trying to add flexibility to the way it allocates budget, moving to a model that is more rolling in nature. In the new process that they have been deploying, Pearson allocates money to projects throughout the year, a process governed by what it calls *product councils*. The councils meet quarterly to make investment decisions and convene monthly to monitor the projects they've funded.

Product councils are distributed, operating within each business unit. They are made up of leadership from those business units, typically director- and VP-level leaders. Each council is cross-functional and includes leaders from technology, product management, finance, strategy, efficacy (responsible for learning outcomes), and other key functions. Notably, the councils do not include senior executives, because they're likely to be too far removed from the day-to-day operations to be able to make informed decisions. Instead, senior executives set strategy and set the overall goals for the councils to meet.

The councils make funding decisions around what Pearson calls its *global product life cycle,* a structure it's been implementing since 2013 to provide a consistent, repeatable, and scalable framework for making product investment decisions. This model is not dissimilar to the three horizon model used at Intuit (described in chapter 5). At Pearson, the life cycle has six phases instead of three, but the fundamental concepts are similar. Early-stage ideas are funded with small investments and are expected to return learning rather than financial results. In other words, teams are asked to validate their business ideas and not to return a profit. Once an idea has been validated, the product council will invest additional funds and will expect more-traditional returns.

The product councils give Pearson the ability to allocate money to ideas rapidly and continuously throughout the year. This arrangement allows it to invest when the opportunity arises and to avoid committing to big projects that haven't proven their merit—and limits the risk of overfunding unproven ideas.

"You can't predict the future," Kresojevic told us. "If your only ability to respond is to cut spending in October, then you're not a responsive business. You're not responding in the places where you can create growth, or where you have a new opportunity presenting itself."

Companies are reluctant to tinker with financial governance processes—and rightly so. Careful financial stewardship is foundational to success. Yet the process Pearson is implementing here shows what's possible when a company, even a company that's more than one hundred years old (Pearson was founded in 1844), faces the future and commits to change. It's possible to take one of the most conservative and appropriately risk-averse parts of the operational elements in a business—the financial governance process—and re-invent it to better fit into the information age.

Avoiding the Shiny Object Syndrome: Sense and Respond and Continuous Marketing

A few years ago, we had the opportunity to work with a manager at a large financial services company. This firm, which provides products and services for consumers and businesses, approached us to create a new website. As we began to work together, however, it became clear that the concept for the project was flawed and that, although we could design and build and launch the product, our research was showing that customers just weren't interested.

Instead, our client, with the approval of the executive she reported to, chose to pivot—to pursue another idea. This idea, one that had been sitting on the back burner in the organization for a while, also proved to have little value. This is the nature of innovation work. You try idea after idea, and mostly you work your way through failure after failure. But we were working quickly and efficiently through a backlog of ideas, and our client was happy—until the end of the project, that is, when we shared our results with her boss. He looked incredulous. "You haven't built anything?" he objected. "I thought you were going to build an app!"

This is *shiny object syndrome*, and it's more common than most of us would like to believe. We get attached to an idea, and, no matter how much rational evidence we gather, we remain convinced that the idea is a good one. We want to unwrap the final product like a Christmas present under the tree. We want the thing.

Marketers know the power of the shiny object, too. Alfred P. Sloan, the legendary head of General Motors, began in the mid-1920s to use the power of annual design and styling changes to create consumer demand for GM cars. And with that stroke of genius, the model year was born. Each year, auto manufacturers reveal "this year's model," a new version of last year's car with just enough improvements to entice consumers, keep prices high, and keep the market engaged. This practice is now standard in the auto industry and has become central to marketing practice. But in a sense and respond world, it becomes harder to make your new product and its features the center of your campaign. It takes time and planning to execute big campaigns. How can you do that when you don't know what's coming? And how can you create big campaigns when changes don't come once a year but are instead delivered in small, frequent increments?

With command and control approaches, you plan what you'll produce and then commit to that plan far in advance. This gives sales and marketing time to plan their campaigns and build materials around the thing you've promised to deliver. But with sense and respond, this kind of planning is rarely possible. This uncertainty can lead to a lot of friction. But there are ways around it that leverage the strengths that marketing and sales departments already have. After all, marketing and sales organizations are already in the business of engaging the market in two-way conversations. Here are a few tactics that we've seen in action:

- *Marketing can become part of the team.* Sense and respond teams face uncertainty about positioning, branding, and messaging. What's the most effective way to talk about the product or service we're offering? How can we communicate the benefits? How can we get people excited? These are questions that teams need to deal with early on, rather than after the fact. By bringing marketing into the core team, you let teams run experiments that address the offering broadly, from features and functions to positioning, brand, and messaging.

- *Marketing can adopt sense and respond methods on its own.* Even when marketing is working independently, team members can benefit from sense and respond approaches. Marketing is increasingly dominated by online channels, and the uncertainty that applies to products and services applies to marketing campaigns as well. Sophisticated marketers have long known how to test campaigns and quantify the impact of their work. These approaches are now both easier and more appropriate than ever before.

- *Marketing can move away from selling products and features and toward campaigns built on brand and benefits.* The features we launch today will evolve significantly in a short amount of time. By focusing efforts on the benefits of the product and service, marketing teams can build agile campaigns without having to spend a lot of time talking about features. In this way, as features come and go, the core message will not change.

- *Road mapping and coordination around big bang campaigns are still possible for larger efforts, but they should be considered the exception rather than the norm.* These kinds of big bang efforts create dependencies that reduce flow and so should be used with caution.

Giving Sales Something to Sell

Sales, too, can find itself out of rhythm when working alongside sense and respond teams. Of course, sales teams vary widely, from people whose jobs are to simply move units to those who work with highly technical, customized sales. The more customized or consultative the sale is, the more opportunity there is, as with marketing, to incorporate it into the core effort of the team.

Outside the customer service department, no one speaks to more customers than members of the sales team. The two-way conversation is how they work. Their insight into what the market is asking for, what the competition is offering, and where the industry is headed is second to none. Their insight can be used as a critical part of the decision-making process about your offering.

However, the incentive structures that drive the sales force often put it at odds with the rest of the teams, especially in a continuous culture. Sales quotas tend to be date driven, and so salespeople may promise certain features by certain dates. This kind of sales-driven product development creates all kinds of problems for product development teams, and, again, these fixed dependencies reduce flow, feedback, and learning.

Salespeople, for their part, can be frustrated by ever-shifting product road maps that make it hard for them to communicate to customers what's coming. Turning the sales dynamic into more of a consultative process seems to be the most promising way to integrate sales into sense and respond teams. When the consultative sale is less appropriate, other measures of sales success, such as delivering great customer service, can be used. The Sonic Automotive teams, covered in chapter 4, are doing exactly this. Instead of focusing on selling the highest-margin vehicles, they focus on a great customer experience. They know that this is their greatest asset and best way to close a sale. Their compensation depends on it. This approach creates a win for both sales and delivery teams, because it helps the delivery teams get firsthand customer insight, and it helps sales create reasons to contact the customer and add value.

Finally, as with marketing, sales teams themselves can benefit from taking up sense and respond. The same test and measure approach that applies in the uncertain worlds of product development and marketing can have tremendous impact in the world of sales.

Eliminating Projects: Continuous Flow and the Project Management Office

Software also tends to make traditional "project" thinking obsolete. When is a piece of software done? The answer is *never.* So instead of organizing "projects" that have a start and end date, agile approaches argue for creating standing teams that own an effort on an ongoing, continuous basis. Thus, instead of chartering a team to build a set of features, we can charter teams to achieve a set of outcomes, as we discuss in chapter 5.

Indeed, this is what has happened at AutoTrader UK, where teams are no longer funded annually to build a set of features. Instead, the organization now checks in with each team on a quarterly basis to see how it's tracking against initiative goals. Initiative goals are quantitative and based on changing customer behavior in some way that benefits the business. Teams get funded to change these behaviors, one quarter at a time. As the quarter nears its end the company assesses, with the team, whether it's worthwhile to continue working toward those outcomes. If so, the team gets another quarter's worth of runway. If not, it moves on to a new initiative.

Sense and Respond Takeaways for Managers

✓ Continuous production, continuous decision making, and continuous learning are the foundations of the sense and respond approach.

✓ As you move from manufacturing to a world of continuous production—as embodied by DevOps, agile, and lean startup—it is important to consider your other business processes and transition them to continuous ones.

✓ Product managers must reconsider release management tactics to control for customer sensitivity, regulatory compliance, seasonality, and cross-team dependencies.

✓ Organizations should use sandboxes to define operation constraints for teams that preserve their freedom of action.

✓ Instead of seeking approval after the fact, teams should seek input from stakeholders as early as possible. Compromises should become part of an operational sandbox for teams.

✓ The annual budgeting process should be reconsidered in favor of more frequent periodic progress checks with teams, based on progress toward business outcomes.

✓ Marketing teams have to adjust to a world in which product features are frequently unknown until just prior to release.

✓ Sales teams must move away from promises about features and dates and toward taking a proactive approach that helps teams understand customer and market needs.

8

Create a Culture of Continuous Learning

A s we discuss briefly in chapter 1, in 1996 the government of Massachusetts set out to build a new digital system linking more than one hundred courthouses across the state. Its goal was to provide a shared database of court records and documents, help court administrators track caseloads, and enable better collaboration between jurisdictions. MassCourts, as the system is known, was initially budgeted at $75 million, and most of it went to Deloitte & Touche, the primary vendor.[1] The system was originally slated to be deployed within five years and handed over to the state for ongoing maintenance and improvements. But in April 2015, the *Boston Globe* broke the story that nineteen years later, the project was still not finished.

Despite the extreme delay, budget overruns (the state had to dip into other funds to complete the project), lack of modern functionality (e.g., the system is not accessible via the web), Deloitte claims it delivered a successful project.[2] One expert witness, Michael Krigsman, testifying before the state legislature, responded, "On which planet can this project be considered a success?"[3]

How could Deloitte claim the project was successful? It comes down to the way IT procurement works. As Krigsman puts it, "To understand . . . we must consider the original contract. Too often, these agreements specify billing based on process milestones rather than customer business outcomes."

That's certainly true in this case: the Commonwealth of Massachusetts set payment milestones based on feature delivery and not on meeting customer needs, usability, or business outcomes. This meant that if Deloitte completed the construction of a feature and it passed the company's quality assurance process, it got paid. And based on those measures it was able to bill and collect the bulk of the $75 million Massachusetts set for the project.

Working on these terms creates a culture that values delivery over success. You can imagine Deloitte's position in this dispute. It set the terms, and Massachusetts agreed. It's sort of like assigning your kid brother to watch the cookie jar. "You said watch them! You didn't say don't eat them!"

Creating Culture

The way you charter work creates culture. If you ask people to build features, they will, and they will value the delivery of those features, even if delivery doesn't create big picture success. They will value the traits and behaviors that make it possible to deliver features. On the other hand, if you ask people to be responsible for success, you are asking them to work in a new way. And although eventually this approach will shape a new culture, that cultural transition needs to be made consciously, and new cultural traits need to be developed and supported.

In other words, changing the way you charter projects is a critical first step, but that change must be accompanied by explicit work on culture.

Reviewing Industrial-Age Command and Control Culture

The command and control culture of the industrial age rewards sticking to the plan—even if you learn that the plan no longer makes sense. Don't ask questions. Don't make waves. Just focus on the task. We call this *delivery culture*. Delivery culture explains why Toyota's practice of *jidoka* seemed radical to the American autoworkers who first encountered it in the 1980s. *Jidoka* is the idea that any production line worker could—indeed was obligated to—stop the line if he or she saw a defect or quality problem. The idea was to fix the problem before it could affect more cars. Only after the problem was fixed could the line be restarted. American workers training alongside Toyota workers in the 1980s were shocked to see this practice in action. The one sacred law of American auto manufacturing was that the line never stopped, no matter what. This moment—when delivery culture met quality culture—encapsulates the challenge organizations face in adopting new values.

A delivery culture that values hitting your production targets and deadline targets is in direct conflict with a culture that prizes discovering and embracing emergent customer value. In a delivery culture there's no time for conversations with the market and no time for learning and iteration. Instead, delivery culture rewards employees and managers for completing tasks on plan rather than confirming that these were the right tasks to complete in the first place.

When you separate the tasks people are performing from the logic that connects those tasks to results, bad things happen. Instead of rewarding thinking, experimenting, problem solving, and learning, you begin to reward order and discipline. In these cultures, mere discussion of the task at hand can be perceived as insubordination. Delivery culture is characterized by top-down decision making, multiyear road maps, annual planning cycles, and arbitrary deadlines. It is not a culture that builds two-way conversations.

It is, therefore, an obsolete and risky way of working in a software-driven world.

Reviewing an Information-Age and Distributed Decision-Making Culture

Instead of a top-down, order-taking culture, sense and respond methods push decision making out into the organization—allowing the people who are closest to the customer, to the markets, and to the situation at hand to make the decisions. It values what these people know, and, even more, it values their ability to learn. With that in mind, we believe there are seven important elements that make up a learning culture.

1. *Humility.* If we don't know what the end looks like, we have to explore to find it.

2. *Permission to fail.* Exploring means that sometimes we'll be wrong. And that's OK.

3. *Self-direction.* As we discover new evidence, we continue to push our learning in the directions we feel will yield the best results.

4. *Transparency.* Transparency means sharing new information—good or bad—broadly so that others may adjust their exploration accordingly.

5. *A bias toward action.* Analysis and thoughtfulness are important, but learning comes from action. We must encourage people to take action and not wait for permission.

6. *Empathy.* Empathy for our customers, users, and peers helps us find value.

7. *Collaboration.* By bringing diverse points of view to bear on a problem, we find better solutions.

Building Element 1: Humility

Kellan Elliott-McCrea, CTO at Etsy from 2011 to 2015, led a pioneering team that many people in the tech world watched with admiration. The Etsy team members were leaders in the DevOps movement and pioneers in the open source community. They introduced numerous techniques that advanced the state of the art. So it's notable that, upon his departure from Etsy, Elliott-McCrea wrote a short essay that focused not on technical accomplishments, but on culture—the culture he helped build during his tenure as CTO.[4] Although his role was technical, the takeaways cut across the entire organization's culture.

The first point Elliott-McCrea makes in the essay is a humble one: he emphasizes the dynamic nature of software when he says, "Nothing we 'know' about software development should be assumed to be true." This is an articulation of perhaps the most important cultural value in a sense and respond world: humility.

It's one thing to know this intellectually. Being humble, though, is the emotional side of this knowledge. It means facing a great deal of pressure from our coworkers, our bosses, and our customers, who want us to have answers and to be certain. Google's first product manager for enterprise products, Rajen Sheth, describes how early customers asked him in 2006 what Google's three-year road map was for its enterprise product suite. Sheth and his team had a vision, but their plan to achieve the vision was filled with uncertainty. After all, no one had ever created a suite of web-based products for the enterprise before, at least not on the scale that Google was planning. The team created a flexible road map, but even that was only a year long. "How could I know what I'll be doing in three years when I'm not even sure what I'll be doing in three months?" Sheth asked.[5]

This is a tough position for a manager to be in. In Sheth's case, he was asking enterprise customers to buy products like email systems that typically have a ten-year life span in an organization. Looking customers in the eye and saying, "I really don't know how we'll get there, but I'm confident that we'll get there"—that's hard. Rather than face this pressure head on, though, few of us do what Sheth did: admit we don't know. Instead, we often choose to make plans, commitments, and budgets. This may seem a better choice in the short term, because these tactics allow us to avoid a difficult conversation, but they frequently backfire in the long run. Customers and stakeholders want to believe that initiatives can be predicted, planned, and budgeted. But when the inevitable happens, when complexity disrupts our careful plans, we are faced with a new problem: reporting the bad news. So great is the pressure to avoid discrepancies between plan and reality that we can close ourselves off from learning entirely. Never mind the problems! Keep the production line running! Hit the deadline!

One manager at a leading financial services firm put it this way: "The struggle is really with traditional product owners who made decisions in one way in the past: these folks are used to being experts. They're used to having the answer. And they've had career success up until now working this way. These folks have a hard time making decisions in a new way, a way that's more of a conversation with customers."

So humility is an important building block of a learning culture. Admitting we don't have all the answers means that we have to find a way to get the answers. We have to figure out how to learn what we need to learn in order to succeed.

Building Element 2: Permission to Fail and a Safe Environment

For a learning culture to thrive, your teams must feel safe to experiment. Experiments are how we learn, but experiments, by nature, fail frequently. In a good experiment, you learn as much from failure as from success. If failure is stigmatized, teams will take few risks.

We once worked with a team at a large financial services organization in the United States to help it learn how to get concepts out of the R&D lab and into the field. In our early meetings, we suggested experiment after experiment. Each suggestion was met with the same response: "Oh, we can't do that here, because . . ." It was frustrating, of course, both for us and for our clients, because we all wanted to work this way. But as frustrating as it was, the team members were correct. They weren't allowed to take the risks associated with the tactics we were proposing, even though these seemed like very small risks to us. One young manager, during a follow-up call a few months later, told us that despite the prohibitions, she had gone ahead with a few small experiments. They had been successful, and her boss celebrated her success—and told her never to do that again!

Sandboxing, discussed in chapter 7, is a way to reduce the risk of experimentation. The idea is to create a set of procedures, rules, and constraints that your organization can live with and within which failure is acceptable. But procedural guidelines are only one part of sandboxing. You also need the cultural permission to experiment. This means creating an understanding with your colleagues and leaders that your progress will not be linear and predictable and that you should not be judged by your *delivery rate* (the amount of stuff you ship) but by your *learning rate*, and by your overall progress toward strategic goals—in other words, by the extent to which you achieve the outcomes in question.

One culture-building practice that organizations use to create permission to fail is the *blameless postmortem*. This regularly occurring meeting provides an opportunity for the entire team to go through a recent time period (product release cycle, quarter, etc.) or to review a specific incident and honestly examine what went well, what could be improved, and what should not be continued. Often, these postmortems are facilitated by someone outside the team to avoid any bias or conflict of interest. Think of this activity as continuous improvement but applied to the way the team works rather than the product it's working on.

The motivation for this process is that failures should be treated as learning opportunities. In order to learn from failures, you need to make an accurate assessment of what happened, why it happened, and how it can be prevented next time. It would be simple to treat this inquiry as a hunt for the person responsible so that this person can be disciplined. But if this is the outcome of the inquiry, then the people involved will not be motivated to share the truth of what happened. Instead, they will cover it up to avoid punishment. So, in order for people to learn, the blameless postmortem process must include an ironclad guarantee that they can speak without fear of punishment. And that guarantee must be upheld each and every time.

Sandboxes, blameless postmortems, and other safe-to-fail learning tactics mitigate the *big* risks organizations face. They allow teams to learn and to respond to changing conditions. They do this by encouraging *small* amounts of risk. It's a trade-off that many organizations find difficult to accept. Instead, many organizations push toward increased process control in order to mitigate *all* risks. This approach mixes up different kinds of risk. It sees small operational risks and seeks to control them absolutely, while remaining blind to the big existential risks. When you increase operational process control, you decrease the freedom your teams experience. As your teams believe they have less freedom to deviate from "standard" processes, they will become less curious and seek increasingly safer solutions. It means they are likely to stay the same, even as markets shift, technology improves, and new paradigms emerge that challenge your position.

Building Element 3: Self-Direction and Alignment

Netflix, another company that takes a very proactive approach to creating and managing culture, opposes these kinds of process controls as a core tenet of the way it operates, declaring, "Process brings seductively strong near-term outcomes."[6] As an alternative, Netflix values hiring responsible people and giving them permission to operate within constraints, with permission to fail, and thus it creates the opportunity for the individuals and the organization to grow and evolve.

In many ways, this approach embodies the work of Douglas McGregor's famous theory X and theory Y of management.[7] McGregor, a management professor in the mid-twentieth century and author of *The Human Side of Enterprise*, proposed that there are at least two discrete ways that managers think about employees and that these assumptions translate directly into management approaches. Theory X proposes that employees dislike work and that the only way to get them to deliver their work is through explicit control, direction, and threats. No sensing. No responding. No learning. This theory holds that employees will shun responsibility, avoid taking the initiative, and relish the explicit direction and tight controls that management can provide.

Theory X describes a worldview held by many managers in industrial-age businesses. In a predictable world where the manufacturing, cost, and use of your product are well known, theory X management was perceived as the right culture. Theory X holds that employees can't be trusted to make good decisions. This makes it consistent with top-down management, in which managers do the thinking, and workers do the labor. There may in fact be places where this management approach makes sense, although the success of the Toyota production system, which introduced thinking and decision making back into the production line, would argue against this approach.

Nevertheless, for information workers, thinking and decision making *are* the work. And, in a learning culture, we all become information workers. In this world theory X-style controls will drive an organization toward irrelevance faster than anything else.

In contrast to theory X, McGregor describes theory Y, a worldview based on Maslow's hierarchy of needs. Theory Y proposes that security and fear are not the only motivators for employees. Instead, theory Y holds that self-direction, alignment with a greater mission, and a desire to improve society are what drive performance, results, and innovation. It's in situations where the mission is clear and the organization is aligned around it that self-direction takes root and delivers superior outcomes. Workers who are self-directed will want to take personal responsibility for quality, collaboration, creativity, and learning.

This is what makes alignment with mission so important in a sense and respond world. Workers need to understand the mission, understand what it means to them, and see how their work connects to and contributes to achieving the mission.

The preference for theory Y-style approaches is pervasive in the software world and reflected in the Agile Manifesto. One of the principles of the manifesto states, "Build projects around motivated individuals. Give them the environment and support they need, and trust them to get the job done."[8]

Building Element 4: Transparency

In the early 2000s, Nokia stood at the apex of the mobile phone world. Before the advent of the smartphone—the first iPhone shipped in 2007—Nokia was the undisputed leader. And yet it faltered badly. It was unable to respond effectively to the changes in the market, and a mere seven years after the iPhone's release, in 2014, Nokia sold its mobile phone business to Microsoft. That business continues to struggle, though. By the end of 2015, it accounted for only about 1 percent of global smartphone sales.[9] What happened?

A recent study by Quy Huy and Timo Vuori, professors of strategy at the European business school INSEAD, argues that the failure was rooted in "shared fears among [Nokia's] middle and top managers [that] led to companywide inertia and left it powerless to respond to Apple's game changing device."[10] In this study, the authors uncovered a pattern in which both "temperamental leaders and frightened middle managers [were] scared of telling the truth." As a result, leaders at the top of the organization were not able to develop an accurate picture of the reality on the ground. Middle managers either kept bad news quiet or explicitly lied to leadership about the state of the work.

As a result of hearing only good news, top managers became even more demanding in terms of technical ambition and target dates for delivery. But these demands were unrealistic, because the teams were already far behind. As a result, product quality slipped to the point that Nokia, once a technical powerhouse, had to resort to sourcing its smartphone operating system externally.

The ancient Greek playwright Sophocles wrote, "For no one loves the messenger who brings bad news." So we've known for at least that long that there's a temptation to blame the messenger. And yet, this only serves to starve the king of the information he needs to rule. So it is with information flow in our organizations. It leads, at least it did at Nokia, to what Huy calls a "pluralistic silence" in which no one was willing to speak the truth that, if accepted, might actually have saved Nokia's smartphone business. In order to thrive in an information age, we need information. Thus, organizations that promote transparency—the honest sharing of information—are the ones that will thrive.

Mike Bland, formerly of Google and currently a practice leader at 18F, the new digital service organization in the US government, wrote recently about the importance of transparency in his experience, first at Google and more recently in the government. Bland describes his motivations for building a web-based information hub to help people at 18F find each other, discover what other people are working on, and share knowledge. He wrote, "We believe that *how* we work is just as important as *what* we produce for our partners. Product is a reflection of process. By setting an example of an open, thriving learning organization, 18F provides an example that members of other federal agencies can use to introduce similar methods into their teams."[11]

Building Element 5: A Bias toward Action

If you've been in any organization for more than a short time, you know that there are certain subjects that come up for debate over and over. You sometimes hear these topics called "religious wars," because they have a quality of ongoing struggle in which each side believes with absolute certainty that it is correct. When these topics come up, you can sometimes hear the less partisan in your organization groan, "Here we go again."

These kinds of debates tend to paralyze groups, and it's important to avoid them. One of the core process points of sense and respond teams is that you'll be making many small decisions, seeking feedback, evaluating the evidence, and then deciding once again how to move forward. And you can't do this quickly if you're constantly debating and analyzing the data. In fact, lengthy, repetitive debate is often a symptom that you don't have enough evidence. In those cases, you need to take action that will generate more evidence, create insight, and allow the team to learn its way forward. You need to initiate a two-way conversation with the market.

Uncertainty is our enemy and obstacle. As we've already argued, in the information age we cannot always accurately predict the effect our actions will have. We cannot use Newtonian math to predict the behavior of our software products. Instead, we have to try things, test ideas, probe. In short, in order to move forward and gain clarity, we must act.

One of the principles we wrote about in our first book, *Lean UX*, was that teams need to prioritize making over analysis. We encouraged product teams to make *something*—a prototype, an experiment, a customer interview—to get the information they were missing, rather than sit around the conference room debating the validity of an idea.

The same approach works at the management level. As the way your company works shifts in response to the uncertainty technology brings, management must adopt a bias toward action, toward experiments that create the data you need to make decisions.

Building Element 6: Empathy and Customer Value

A few years ago, design researcher Jared Spool studied teams to see what effect exposure to customers had on product success. According to the study he published in 2011, teams that met with real customers for at least two hours per team member every six weeks produced superior products.[12] In the study, Spool calls this key metric *exposure hours*, or the number of hours that each member of the team is exposed to customers. This last point is important. Teams that do a lot of research but in which only research specialists participate do not see this improvement in product quality. The second key point in the study is that the research can't be done only once. It has to be done continuously; the study found a frequency of at least every six weeks to be the magic number.

In other words, repeated exposure to customers struggling with real-life problems, in the field, drove more empathic conversations and helped teams focus on solutions that added customer value.

Sense and respond approaches consider customer value as the necessary path to achieve business value, and so they place customer value at the core of everything the organization does. This means that the organization must build and maintain high levels of empathy for the customers it is serving. Everyone from the CEO to the call-center representatives must have a sense of what your customers are trying to achieve, what's getting in their way, and how your solutions help them overcome those obstacles. Empathy helps us find a path through uncertainty. It pokes holes in our assumptions about our customers and their needs. It grounds us in their reality.

Sometimes customer empathy is your company's only chance of maintaining a strong market position in the face of global competition. This was the situation in which Maxdome, a German video streaming service, found itself in 2015. Maxdome was facing two major challenges. First, the German market is generally skeptical of subscription services. Increasing the pressure, both Netflix and Amazon Prime were on track for local launches in the immediate future. A subsidiary of the German-language mass media conglomerate ProsiebenSat.1, Maxdome decided to reinvent its service—and the company culture—from the ground up.

Maxdome CEO Marvin Lange knew he couldn't win a feature-based arms race against well-funded rivals like Netflix and Amazon Prime.[13] So rather than give his teams a list of features to start developing, Lange gave them a strategic challenge—a mission: to win by being the best at "video discovery" and "content inspiration." This would be the goal of the service. The firm wouldn't measure progress in terms of features built. Instead, the benchmarks would be customer acquisition, service usage, and retention.

To figure out how inspiration and discovery would manifest, Lange gave his teams one more challenge: to get to know their customers. Lange told us that an organization that understands the needs, pain points, and cultural eccentricities of its customers will ultimately build a superior service. "We as a management team now always challenge everyone to do real user testing on everything, and to put the customer first," Lange told us. "Sounds very basic, but it's not." Lange has rolled out five tactics to achieve this.

First, he has required every manager to take customer service calls once a month. The managers' job is to experience the front lines of customer frustration. What's driving the phone calls? Where is the product failing? What are the opportunities to improve? Maxdome's managers could easily receive this information in a monthly report, but the discomfort of hearing it directly from customers helps ensure that these concerns don't get lost in feature prioritization discussions.

Second, each year around the holiday season, Maxdome's managers try to sell their service on busy shopping streets around Germany. This scenario goes one step further than listening in on support calls. Managers aren't just seeking customer input or complaints; they are actively trying to convince random passersby to purchase the service on the spot. (We've talked throughout the book about the two-way conversation with the market. Sometimes, we've meant this metaphorically, but in this case, managers are having literal conversations with their customers.) The managers try out different on-the-street sales tactics to see what works. The pitches and concepts that convert strangers into customers on the street are the ones managers will integrate into marketing and advertising, and into product development work, in the coming year.

Maxdome's third initiative is to provide an unlimited budget for customer exposure. Anyone in the organization can set up conversations or user experience studies with customers to determine how (or whether) to move an initiative forward. The only requirement is that the learning from these studies be made broadly available and that the insight the studies yield be used in decision making. Since Lange established this program in 2015, Maxdome is running studies at a pace of about forty to fifty per year.

Fourth, Maxdome has started a process it calls "dogfooding." Derived from the phrase "eating your own dogfood," this is the process of company employees using the service they are building on a regular basis for their own downtime entertainment. Nothing will motivate a manager of a team to design and develop an intuitive and usable video discovery feature like having his three-year-old screaming for her favorite cartoon as Dad fumbles through clunky menu structures, slow search results, and poor content choices.

Maxdome's final initiative is knowledge transfer. Every month, the firm holds an all-hands meeting where the customer insights people have gathered are shared broadly. They discuss the new behavior patterns they are seeing and consider how these patterns might affect product plans. In addition, Lange always shares a few short video clips of managers doing their time in the call center. This helps drive home the point that empathy is a companywide concern.

Ultimately what these tactics illustrate is Maxdome's dedication to building a culture of continuous learning through customer empathy. Teams constantly evaluate plans as new customer insight arrives and continuously shift their effort in increasingly accurate directions. Their barometer for success is customer behavior. If they can positively impact it, they report that as a success. If not, they report it as learning, not failure, and quickly assess how to make the next effort better.

This approach has helped Maxdome in areas beyond product quality. Not surprisingly, when people are able to do higher-quality work, their satisfaction increases, and this is what Maxdome is seeing. Since it has started these programs, Lange reports that the number of Maxdome employees who would recommend Maxdome as an employer has doubled, from 35 percent to roughly 70 percent.

Building Element 7: Collaboration, Diversity, and Trust

In 1959, musician Miles Davis assembled his sextet to record a new album he called *Kind of Blue*. The musicians gathered with almost no idea what they were to play and without any rehearsal. Davis was at the height of his career, but he was also becoming frustrated with bebop, the style of jazz he had been working in for a decade. He had been experimenting with a new style, *modal jazz*, and for *Kind of Blue*, he wanted to go all in.

Over the course of only two days the band recorded what was to become the best-selling jazz record of all time and what many people consider the greatest jazz recording ever. One critic wrote, "*Kind of Blue* isn't merely an artistic highlight for Miles Davis, it's an album that towers above its peers, a record generally considered as the definitive jazz album, a universally acknowledged standard of excellence."[14] How was this possible? What was the culture Davis created during those sessions that allowed that creativity to happen?

In his 2011 TED talk, Stefon Harris, himself an accomplished jazz musician, noted that there are "no mistakes on the bandstand."[15] Instead, he said, every note played is an opportunity to move the "product" forward in a new direction, but only if you're listening to what your bandmates are doing and are prepared to seize the opportunities that their playing creates for you. Harris makes the case that this collaboration and listening, and this willingness to embrace what your colleagues are doing, is what allows jazz improvisation to happen.

Jazz is improvised music. It can't be predicted, written down, or precisely scripted in advance. Improvised music is an interplay between freedom and constraints. Musicians obey certain constraints—a key, a rhythm, a set of chord changes—that keep them together. But they also have freedom to explore—to make decisions within those constraints. What we call "mistakes" happen when musicians inadvertently step outside a constraint. They play a note outside the given key, or they step out of the tempo. An alert band of collaborators can catch this moment and turn it into an opportunity. They accept the new note, they understand it implies moving to a new key, and they, in that moment, decide to move in that direction.

This was Davis's secret sauce. He was a master improviser and had been collaborating with these musicians for years. So even as he changed from bebop to modal jazz, what he was really doing was changing the constraints. The underlying working process—the collaboration, the listening, the improvisational skills—these hadn't really changed. Davis provided the vision in the form of "sketches" for each song. This was like strategy—the high-level direction for the band. However, he had the humility to leave the execution to the other players' individual brilliance. Davis created a space where the best ideas emerged from the talented team that he hired—Bill Evans, John Coltrane, Cannonball Adderley, Paul Chambers, and Jimmy Cobb. Davis's sketches set the direction, but the instrumentalists built the music together. A piano solo here, a saxophone accent there. They listened to each other. The music became a conversation with peaks and valleys, shape and form.

Collaboration is critical to sense and respond approaches. It starts with the idea that a small team, working in short, iterative cycles will need diverse skills. There's no time for lengthy, sequential work with hand-offs between specialists. We write about this in detail in chapter 6, but we want to spend a few more moments with the idea here, because there's a cultural component to collaboration that allows the process to happen.

One of the things that makes collaboration so powerful is that it combines people with different points of view and different skills to work on a problem together. The challenge, of course, is that the same thing that makes diversity so powerful can also serve as the root of conflict: different people have different values, make different assumptions, have different biases and prejudices, and bring different knowledge to the table. To turn this mix into a productive team rather than a free-for-all, you need to create some shared purpose, and you need to create trust.

This was certainly true for Thomas Edison at his famous laboratory in Menlo Park, New Jersey. Edison, along with his employees, often stayed late in the lab to work on experiments. During these late evening hours, Edison was known to host what he called "midnight lunch," convening his employees for dinner, storytelling, even singing and playing music together. These sessions helped everyone get past the work and the role definitions and get to know each other as people.[16] This type of activity creates a baseline of trust to draw on when, for example, an engineer and a product manager come into conflict over some feature.

The importance of social ties is something we sometimes forget, but it comes up repeatedly when people talk about creative teams. In a recent article on building productive design studios, designers Rhys Newman and Luke Johnson lay out fifteen principles for a good design studio, and many of them have to do with building good social ties across the team. Say "Good morning" and "Good night," for example, to start building a courteous social culture. Laugh more to deflate conflict and draw people closer together. Eat and cook together to encourage people to let their guard down; be vulnerable and human together. Meet out in the open to encourage trust and openness. Bring the outside in, or share family life and outside interests with one another, again, to become more human in one another's eyes. These are great practices for any team, not only for design studios, because they create an atmosphere in which collaboration is possible.[17]

Embracing Change Means Embracing Culture Change

How do you change culture? This is a question for which there are no easy answers, and a topic of never-ending debate for managers, consultants, and experts. There's no shortage of opinion. "Culture is conversations," one expert declares. Another pundit writes, "Culture is what you do, not what you say." Still a third claims, "Culture is what you do when the CEO isn't in the room." They may all be right to some degree—in other words, these ideas may not conflict but may merely reflect different parts of the whole. Culture building, like much of what we talk about in this book, is rife with uncertainty.

So where do you start? We think that an important first step, perhaps not surprisingly, is to embrace the idea that culture, like everything else, is in a constant state of change. Shani Hilton, deputy editor in chief at BuzzFeed, told a reporter, "We're still in a state of figuring things out. We're into change, we're used to it, we're down with it. The bigger we get, the harder it is to get people to realize: We don't have to do things the way we've done them for the last six months."[18]

And John Borthwick, a venture capitalist and entrepreneur who runs Betaworks, an innovation incubator in New York, put it this way: "Each change, each innovation is considered to be the new normal, a new steady state when in fact the new normal is a state of continual innovation."[19]

Culture change certainly comes from doing new things. This action-centered view of culture creation come from the idea that culture is what you do. The Maxdome story shows that by encouraging people to do new things, you can create new perceptions and new points of view, and from there you can add new elements to a culture. To get people doing new things—and the things you want—you need leadership.

In other words, culture change must be led. Embracing change as a cultural value starts at the highest levels of the organization. It starts with transparency and humility at the board and C-suite levels. It impacts the way we structure our conversations with the rest of the company and is reflected in the way we communicate with the organization. Here, for example, is how Dean Baquet, editor in chief at the *New York Times*, shared his plans for the future of the newsroom there.

In ways large and small, the newsroom is experimenting and adapting as we move into our digital future . . .

We are . . . beginning to free desks to focus on coverage without being consumed by print deadlines. We have begun a desk-by-desk digital training regimen. We have gone from being largely unaware of our audience's changing habits to making them an integral part of our daily conversations . . .

We debate openly and freely as we experiment with new ways of telling stories.

Anyone who compares today's version of The Times to a version from the good old days quickly sees how much stronger today's is. My goal is to ensure that our successors will edit a report that is better yet.[20]

So much of what we've discussed in this chapter is present in this memo. A willingness to experiment. An openness to debate. An emphasis on empathy. And an embrace of continuous change.

Making Culture Everyone's Priority

Culture doesn't come only from the top. In fact, you can't impose culture on an organization, at least not without inflicting a great deal of collateral damage. Zappos founder Tony Hsieh tried this in 2015 by forcing his fourteen hundred employees to adopt holocracy—a management style that eschews managers and process in favor of autonomous collectives. Hsieh declared that anyone who didn't want to work in the new system could take a severance package and leave. Some published reports say that as many as 18 percent of the workforce may have taken this option, and many of those who chose to stay suffered through a period of morale challenges and feelings of betrayal.[21]

Instead, it seems more productive to embrace a meeting of both top-down and bottom-up culture change initiatives. This echoes the pattern we see throughout sense and respond approaches. People are working in new ways. Pay attention to these new behaviors. Support and amplify them, and support the culture leaders who are leading the way. Create a feedback loop inside your organization in which a new culture can emerge. Support what's happening organically, and create probes and tests to encourage more of what you want to develop. You might not know in advance what you're looking for, but when you see it, you might recognize it and then be able to build on it.

Kellan Elliott-McCrea, in the same essay we cited earlier, went on to say this: "You build a culture of learning by optimizing globally not locally. Your improvement, over time, as a team, with shared tools, practices and beliefs is more important than individual pockets of brilliance. And more satisfying." What he is intimating is that continuous improvement isn't the work of one person. It's not the responsibility of one department. It has to be a shared organizational priority.

Sense and Respond Takeaways for Managers

✓ Sense and respond approaches are not only about process changes. They are equally about building a learning culture.

✓ The key elements of a learning culture are humility, permission to fail, self-direction, transparency, a bias toward action, empathy, and collaboration.

✓ Managers must embody these values and support them where they emerge in the organization.

✓ Culture change is rife with uncertainty. Culture is in effect a product of your organization's ongoing conversation with itself about itself. So approach it with a sense and respond mindset. Observe what's working, amplify it, and don't be afraid to experiment.

Conclusion

This is a remarkable moment in the world economy, a moment of unique changes made possible by digital technology. These changes present us all with both unprecedented threats and, if we can act, welcome opportunities. And, as the change is taking place around us at this very moment, much of the story remains unwritten. It is up to us to see the changes and respond to them as best we can. Some of these responses already have been discovered to work. We've done our best to describe them in this book, and hopefully it will give you a starting point.

There are other responses waiting to be discovered, tried, and tested. Some of what you try will work, and some won't. That's the nature of innovation, and we hope we've made clear that this process of trial and error is both our only reasonable tactic and our best way forward.

Either way, this transformation is coming. The need to evolve is here. Organizations that hope to thrive will need to evolve, and doing so will require leadership. Make no mistake: the transformation must be led. Although the organic, bottom-up desire to change needs to be there from your teams, in our experience this is not likely to be a problem. People want to work in a new way. No, instead, it's now up to leadership. It's time to give up the comfort we find in the way it's always been done and embrace the new ideas and methods of the sense and respond world.

Changing with the Changing World

The driver of all this change is digital technology. This is the new material on which your business is built. This material is unlike the materials we used in the twentieth century, and it requires new business processes to harness its power and its complexity. Using our old command and control methods, methods we inherited from physical manufacturing, is not only ineffective but also dangerous. These methods ignore the complexity that is inherent in digital services and the uncertainty they create. They create false expectations. They prevent us from discovering value, learning how to exploit it, and improving our ability to deliver it. To thrive in the digital age, we must move away from command and control and move to sense and respond methods. Our competitors are already making this move. Large incumbents are being swallowed by smaller players who take sense and respond methods as their birthright.

Sense and respond methods rely on a continuous feedback loop—an ongoing conversation (both metaphorical and literal) between our organizations and the people they serve. This conversation helps us figure out what our customers value, and it helps them express what they value. It allows us to try things out, see what works, and adjust until we find the sweet spot: something that creates value for both our customers and our business. This way of working, of navigating uncertainty, has been developed in parallel across many disciplines.

We see these continuous, feedback-based processes in methods like agile, DevOps, design thinking, and lean startup. Taken together, this body of methods is the future, and our challenge now is to look at our organizations and institutions and evolve them—or risk seeing them replaced by newcomers.

Running Companies by Last Century's Rules

The changes required will go deep. As we've discussed, they cut across every department and function in an organization. Finance will need to reassess the way budgets are made. Product management will need to reassess road maps and portfolio planning. Marketing and sales must move from a predictable, feature-based world into a world of continuous value creation and delivery. "This year's model" is a thing of the past.

Legal teams and compliance teams will need to work with delivery teams to find safe ways to enable continuous learning. In other words, technology is no longer only an IT problem. The rhythm of technology is changing the rhythm of business, and we're all going to need to adapt.

Getting Started with Principles, Tools, and Stories

The good news is that there are companies and institutions out there doing it. There are principles available to study, a wealth of tools at your disposal, and, as we've tried to bring you in this book, stories of both success and failure that you can use as a guide. In fact, one of the great advantages of this particular moment is that the digital culture tends to be open by default. At the practitioner level, communities have grown around sharing methods to deal with this change, so help from your peers is readily available. You just have to seek out your community of peers, whether it be the Beyond Budgeting Round Table for CFOs or one of the agile working groups that have sprung up for marketers, lawyers, and so on.

Remember in all of this, the key principles remain the same: a two-way conversation based on learning, continuous flow, and a customer-centered definition of value must take priority over following a predetermined plan of action. Cross-functional collaboration must lead the structure of the organization.

Grasping That It Isn't Easy

We have no illusions that it is easy to make these changes. And we can't tell you *how* to change. Change happens in an organization according to the unique attributes found there. It happens when visionary leaders recognize the change around them and rally their colleagues to the cause. But looking at what others are doing, and what others have found that works well, serves as a strong starting point. For every Netflix that has embraced change from the beginning, there is a Blockbuster that has failed to create the adaptability it needs in order to survive.

Finding That the Payoff Is Worth It

We've seen what it's like inside thriving organizations, and we hope we've painted a vivid picture of it for you here. These organizations are learning organizations. They are not afraid to try and to fail, because they know that's how they learn, and through learning they find success. The people there are engaged in the learning. They find individual growth and satisfaction, and they wrestle individually and in groups with the challenges they face. They find new ways to success, and they share these with the rest of the organization. And, with a taste of this culture, they are loath to go back to the old ways of working.

Learning to Evolve

We hope you'll take this book as a call to arms. We want you to pick one or two of the methods you've seen here and try them at your workplace. Grab a colleague and start a discussion. Talk with your team about what's possible to change within your group. Talk with your boss about how you might adopt some of these approaches. Speak with your vendors and your clients and your customers to see where you can get a foothold on this path. We hope you can start this journey with a learner's mindset. There will be failure and success, and hopefully you can embrace them both.

Finally, we—Jeff and Josh—hope that you will stay in touch with us and share what you learn on your journey. We've done our best in this book to share what we've learned so far in our work, but we know that our learning is far from complete. We'll continue to do this work and meet people and companies that are confronting these changes, and we'll continue to report on what we find. You can always reach us at jeff@jeffgothelf.com and josh@joshuaseiden. com. Please get in touch, and good luck!

Notes

Introduction

1. James Estrin, "Kodak's First Digital Moment," *New York Times*, August 12, 2015, http://lens.blogs.nytimes.com/2015/08/12/kodaks-first-digital-moment/; Michael Zang, "This Is What the History of Camera Sales Looks Like with Smartphones Included," *PetaPixel*, April 9, 2015, http://petapixel.com/2015/04/09/this-is-what-the-history-of-camera-sales-looks-like-with-smartphones-included/; Dawn McCarty and Beth Jinks, "Kodak Files for Bankruptcy as Digital Era Spells End to Film," *Bloomberg Technology*, January 19, 2012, http://www.bloomberg.com/news/articles/2012-01-19/kodak-photography-pioneer-files-for-bankruptcy-protection-1-.

2. Maltzberger, "Kindle Is the Fire That Burns Brightest for Amazon," SeekingAlpha.com, March 8, 2013, http://seekingalpha.com/article/1259661-kindle-is-the-fire-that-burns-brightest-for-amazon-com.

3. Kasra Ferdows, Michael A. Lewis, and Jose A.D. Machuca, "Zara's Secret to Fast Fashion," Harvard Business School Working Knowledge, February 21, 2005, http://hbswk.hbs.edu/archive/4652.html.

4. Michael Schrage, "R&D, Meet E&S (Experiment and Scale)," *MIT Sloan Management Review* blog, May 11, 2016, http://sloanreview.mit.edu/article/rd-meet-es-experiment-scale/?utm_source=twitter&utm_medium=social&utm_campaign=sm-direct.

Chapter 1

1. "The Trust Engineers," Radiolab, February 9, 2015, www.radiolab.or/story/trust-engineers.

2. Jon Jenkins, "Velocity Culture," 2011, https://www.youtube.com/watch?v=dxk8b9rSKOo.

3. Chris Doig, "Enterprise Software Project Success Remains Elusive," CIO.com, October 23, 2015, http://www.cio.com/article/2996716/enterprise-software/why-is-success-with-enterprise-software-projects-so-elusive.html.

4. Jared M. Spool, "The $300 Million Button," User Interface Engineering, January 14, 2009, https://articles.uie.com/three_hund_million_button/.

5. Scout Addis, Obama for America campaign worker, personal interview, 2015.

6. Shea Bennett, "The History of Hashtags in Social Media Marketing," *AdWeek* blog, September 2, 2014, http://www.adweek.com/socialtimes/history-hashtag-social-marketing/501237.

7. David J. Snowden and Mary E. Boone, "A Leader's Framework for Decision Making," *Harvard Business Review*, November 2007, https://hbr.org/2007/11/a-leaders-framework-for-decision-making.

8. Etsy.com, "Etsy, Inc. Reports Fourth Quarter and Full Year 2015 Financial Results," press release, February 23, 2016, http://investors.etsy.com/phoenix.zhtml?c=253952&p=irol-newsArticle&ID=2142373.

9. *Consumer Reports*, Twitter post, March 19, 2015, 9:27 am, https://twitter.com/CRcars/status/578593771337682944.

Chapter 2

1. Eric Ries, *The Lean Startup: How Today's Entrepreneurs Use Continuous Innovation to Create Radically Successful Businesses* (New York: Crown Business, 2001).

2. "In-App Purchase for Developers," Apple, Inc., accessed August 26, 2016, https://developer.apple.com/in-app-purchase/.

3. For example, see Austin Carr, "The Real Story Behind Jeff Bezos's Fire Phone Debacle and What It Means for Amazon's Future," *Fast Company*, January 6, 2015, https://www.fastcompany.com/3039887/under-fire.

4. Ibid.

5. Brian Jackson, "Canadian Tire Money Enters Era of Mobile Payments," ITBusiness.ca, October 29, 2014, http://www.itbusiness.ca/news/canadian-tire-money-enters-era-of-mobile-payments/51907.

6. Ed Catmull with Amy Wallace, *Creativity, Inc.: Overcoming the Unseen Forces That Stand in the Way of True Inspiration* (New York: Random House, 2014), Kindle edition, loc. 143.

7. Fiona Graham, "Searching the Internet's Long Tail and Finding Parrot Cages," BBC News, October 7, 2010, http://www.bbc.com/news/business-11495839.

8. Ibid.

Chapter 3

1. *Driving Digital Transformation: New Skills for Leaders, New Role for the CIO*, Harvard Business Review Analytic Services Report, 2015, https://enterprisersproject.com/sites/default/files/Driving%20Digital%20Transformation:%20New%20Skills%20for%20Leaders,%20New%20Role%20for%20the%20CIO.pdf.

2. Associated Press, "A Win for Uber: Car-Service Apps Can Update without City Approval," June 22, 2015, http://www.crainsnewyork.com/article/20150622/TRANSPORTATION/150629988.

3. Andrea Rothman, "Airbus Builds Innovation Labs for Faster Tech Advances," Bloomberg, March 9, 2015, http://skift.com/2015/03/09/airbus-builds-innovation-labs-for-faster-tech-advances/.

4. GOV.UK, "About the Government Digital Service," Government Digital Service blog, accessed September 1, 2016, https://gds.blog.gov.uk/about/.

5. Noah Kunin, Twitter post, December 12, 2014, 6:22 p.m., https://twitter.com/noahkunin/status/543591687084589056; ibid., 6:24 p.m., https://twitter.com/noahkunin/status/543592161951121409; and ibid., 6:25 p.m., https://twitter.com/noahkunin/status/543592503778484224.

6. GOV.UK, "How the Alpha Phase Works," accessed September 1, 2016, https://www.gov.uk/service-manual/phases/alpha.html.

7. Amy Wilson et al., "Two Agencies Participating in the Digital Acquisition Accelerator Pilot," 18F, June 15, 2016, https://18f.gsa.gov/2016/06/15/two-agencies-participating-in-the-digital-acquisition-accelerator-pilot/.

8. Personal communication, 2015.

Chapter 4

1. Greg Jarboe, "L'Oreal Launches New Makeup Line Designed by YouTube Beauty Guru Michelle Phan," Search Engine Watch, August 19, 2013, https://searchenginewatch.com/sew/study/2289834/loreal-launches-new-makeup-line-designed-by-youtube-beauty-guru-michelle-phan.

2. "Luxury and Cosmetics Financial Factbook 2013," EY.com, accessed September 1, 2016, http://www.ey.com/GL/en/Industries/Consumer-Products/Luxury-and-cosmetics-financial-factbook-2013.

3. Tom Peters, Twitter post, January 2, 2015, 4:23 a.m., https://twitter.com/tom_peters/status/550990859756634113; ibid., 8:33 a.m., https://twitter.com/tom_peters/status/551053682151026688; and ibid., 9:49 a.m., https://twitter.com/tom_peters/status/551072739537461248.

4. Roger Dooley, "Three Customer Loyalty Lessons from Coffee Companies—Only One is Good," *Forbes*, January 7, 2015, http://www.forbes.com/sites/rogerdooley/2015/01/07/coffee-loyalty/.

5. Ben Geier, "Car Dealerships Turn to Ipads, Not Sign Twirlers, to Win Business," *Fortune*, September 2, 2014, http://fortune.com/2014/09/02/car-dealerships-turn-to-ipads-not-sign-twirlers-to-win-business/.

6. Personal interview, Mark Chamberlain, Select Sires director of information services, 2015.

7. Nellie Bowles, "Michelle Phan: From YouTube Star to $84 Million Startup Founder," Recode.com, October 27, 2014, http://www.recode.net/2014/10/27/11632302/michelle-phan-youtube-star-to-startup-founder.

8. The New York Times, *The Full New York Times Innovation Report*, https://www.scribd.com/doc/224608514/The-Full-New-York-Times-Innovation-Report.

9. Ibid., p. 4.

10. Ibid., p. 15.

11. Ibid., p. 32.

12. Reuters, "New York Times Co. Profit Jumps 48% on Digital Growth," February 4, 2016, http://fortune.com/2016/02/04/new-york-times-earnings/?iid=leftrail.

13. Interview with Emily Culp at Rebecca Minkoff; Phil Wahba, "Nordstrom Taps Ebay's Tech to Build Fitting Room of the Future," *Fortune*, November 25, 2014, http://fortune.com/2014/11/25/nordstrom-ebay-fitting-rooms/; Elizabeth Holmes, "Designer Rebecca Minkoff's New Stores Have Touch Screens for an Online Shopping Experience," *Wall Street Journal*, November 11, 2014, http://m.wsj.com/articles/designer-rebecca-minkoffs-new-stores-have-touch-screens-for-an-online-shopping-experience-1415748733?mobile=y; and Billy Steele, "Neiman Marcus' Digital Mirror Compares Clothes Side by Side," Engadget.com, January 13, 2015, http://www.engadget.com/2015/01/13/neiman-marcus-memory-mirror/.

14. Frank Konkel, "The Details about the CIA's Deal with Amazon," *The Atlantic*, July 17, 2014, http://www.theatlantic.com/technology/archive/2014/07/the-details-about-the-cias-deal-with-amazon/374632/.

15. Emily Steel, "Nielsen Plays Catch-Up as Streaming Era Wreaks Havoc on TV Raters," *New York Times*, February 2, 2016, http://www.nytimes.com/2016/02/03/business/media/nielsen-playing-catch-up-as-tv-viewing-habits-change-and-digital-rivals-spring-up.html?_r=0.

16. Rick Porter, "Netflix Says Ratings Estimates 'Remarkably Inaccurate,' Won't Change Its No-Numbers Stance," Zap2it.com, January 17, 2016,

http://tvbythenumbers.zap2it.com/2016/01/17/netflix-says-ratings-estimates-remarkably-inaccurate-wont-change-its-no-numbers-stance/.

17. Mary Meeker, "2015 Internet Trends Report," May 27, 2015, http://www.slideshare.net/kleinerperkins/internet-trends-v1.

18. Dan Farber, "Why Romney's Orca Killer App Beached on Election Day," CNet.com, November 9, 2012, http://www.cnet.com/news/why-romneys-orca-killer-app-beached-on-election-day/.

19. Michael Kranish, "ORCA, Mitt Romney's High-Tech Get-Out-the Vote Program, Crashed on Election Day," Boston.com, http://archive.boston.com/news/politics/2012/president/candidates/romney/2012/11/10/orca-mitt-romney-high-tech-get-out-the-vote-program-crashed-election-day/gflS8VkzDcJcX-CrHoV0nsI/story.html.

20. Farber, "Why Romney's Orca Killer App Beached on Election Day."

Chapter 5

1. Stephen Bungay, *The Art of Action: How Leaders Close the Gaps between Plans, Actions, and Results* (London: Nicholas Brealey Publishing, 2010), Kindle edition.

2. Dan North, "Why Agile Doesn't Scale, and What You Can Do About It," presentation at GOTO conference, September 30, 2013, http://gotocon.com/aarhus-2013/presentation/Why+Agile+doesn't+scale,+and+what+you+can+do+about+it. When we spoke to North, he went on to say, "If you want to scale and be agile, the solution may not be more scrum teams." (Scrum is the most popular agile method. When people think of agile, they're usually thinking of scrum.) Instead, he told us, "When you have a lot of work to do, you have to ask, What is the shape of the work, and what's the best shape of people to do the work?" North described a process of asking these questions quarterly and adjusting assignments and organization *continuously* in response to the nature of the work.

3. TechBeacon, "State of Performance Engineering, 2015–2016 Edition," http://techbeacon.com/sites/default/files/State-of-Performance-Engineering-2015-16_FINAL2.pdf.

4. Bungay, *Art of Action*, loc. 2856.

5. Neil Williams, interview with authors, 2016.

6. Williams told us that the system described here has evolved somewhat in the time they've been using the process. "As we learn, we change things," he told us. Now that GOV.UK is an established platform that's used across government, there is more need to coordinate work across departments. As a

result, the team finds more need to communicate hard dates. Still, Williams told us, plans are subject to change. "It doesn't change the uncertainty," he said, "just how we communicate about it. We tell people, this is the plan, it's the best plan we have, and it will probably change."

7. This is similar to an approach used by the Google Apps team in 2006 and 2007. Team members describe using these same planning buckets, along with one additional bucket, which is the "not doing" bucket. This last category helps stakeholders understand which features are explicitly out of scope. https://library.gv.com/climbing-mount-enterprise-99a4d014f942#.iasj0ux35.

8. Donald Reinertsen, *The Principles of Product Development Flow* (Redondo Beach, CA: Celeritas, 2012), 250.

9. "GOV.UK High-Level Road Map," Trello, https://trello.com/b/Gyq-sETvS/gov-uk-high-level-roadmap.

10. Bungay, *Art of Action*, loc. 923.

11. Mehrdad Baghai, Stephen Coley, and David White, *The Alchemy of Growth* (New York: Basic Books, 2000).

12. This description is based on an interview with Brad Smith, Intuit CEO, by Eric Ries at the Startup Lessons Learned Conference, 2011, http://criticalthinking.tumblr.com/post/6713640477/brad-smith-ceo-intuit-at-startup-lessons.

13. Hugh Molotsi, "Horizon Planning at Intuit," February 14, 2014, http://blog.hughmolotsi.com/2014_02_01_archive.html.

14. Geoffrey Moore, "To Succeed in the Long Term, Focus on the Middle Term," *Harvard Business Review*, July–August 2007, https://hbr.org/2007/07/to-succeed-in-the-long-term-focus-on-the-middle-term.

Chapter 6

1. This formulation is often attributed to author and strategist Larry Keeley. But designer Alan Cooper, who cites Keeley in his book *The Inmates Are Running the Asylum* (Boston: Pearson, 1999), says, "You could make a case that it comes from Vitruvius, just a tad earlier" (Vitruvius, the ancient Roman architect and author, is known for his assertion that architecture must be solid, useful, and beautiful; and personal communication with Alan Cooper.

2. Cian Ó Maidin, "Release the Kraken: How PayPal Is Being Revolutionized by Node.js and Lean-UX," NearForm.com, November 5, 2013, http://www.nearform.com/nodecrunch/release-the-kracken-how-paypal-is-being-revolutionized-by-node-js-and-lean-ux/.

3. Brad Power, "How GE Applies Lean Startup Practices," *Harvard Business Review*, April 23, 2014, https://hbr.org/2014/04/how-ge-applies-lean-startup-practices/.

4. The New York Times, *The Full New York Times Innovation Report*, https://www.scribd.com/doc/224608514/The-Full-New-York-Times-Innovation-Report.

5. Clement Huyghebaert, "What Is It Like to Be an Engineer at BuzzFeed," Quora.com, accessed September 1, 2016, https://www.quora.com/What-is-it-like-to-be-an-engineer-at-BuzzFeed.

6. Vox, "Code of Conduct," accessed September 1, 2016, http://code-of-conduct.voxmedia.com/.

7. Personal communication with Bill Scott, 2015.

8. Eric Savitz, "The Death of Outsourcing, and Other IT Management Trends," Forbes.com, December 28, 2012, http://www.forbes.com/sites/ciocentral/2012/12/28/the-death-of-outsourcing-and-other-it-management-trends/#12657a6775c7; and Stephanie Overby, "Goodbye Outsourcing, Hello Insourcing: A Trend Rises," CIO.com, February 17, 2011, http://www.cio.com/article/2411036/outsourcing/goodbye-outsourcing–hello-insourcing–a-trend-rises.html.

Chapter 7

1. Nathan Coe, interview, 2015.

2. Chris Kelly, interview, 2015.

3. Beyond Budgeting Institute, accessed September 1, 2016, http://www.beyondbudgeting.org/beyond-budgeting/bb-problem.html.

4. Sonja Kresojevic, interview, 2016.

Chapter 8

1. Todd Wallack, "Call It Big Data's Big Dig—$75m, 19 Years, Still Not Done," *Boston Globe*, April 12, 2015, http://www.boston-globe.com/metro/2015/04/11/massachusetts-courts-long-delayed-computer-system-may-leave-public-out/S7tZcbvBDFd3nho7XvEZPO/story.html.

2. Michael Krigsman, "An IT Failure Unicorn: Endless 19-Year Project in Massachusetts," ZDNet, April 13, 2015, http://www.zdnet.com/article/an-it-failure-unicorn-endless-19-year-project-in-massachusetts/.

3. Ibid.

4. Kellan Elliott-McCrea, "Five Years, Building a Culture, and Handing It Off," Medium, August 31, 2015, https://medium.com/@kellan/five-years-building-a-culture-and-handing-it-off-54a38c3ab8de#.cre5m6xat.

5. Ken Norton, "Climbing Mount Enterprise," GV Library, August 5, 2013, https://library.gv.com/climbing-mount-enterprise-99a4d014f942.

6. Reed Hastings, "Process Brings Seductively Strong Near-Term Outcome," SlideShare, August 1, 2009, http://www.slideshare.net/reed2001/culture-1798664/51-Process_Brings_Seductively_Strong_NearTerm.

7. Douglas McGregor, *The Human Side of Enterprise* (New York: McGraw-Hill, 1960).

8. "Manifesto for Agile Software Development," accessed September 1, 2016, www.agilemanifesto.org.

9. Tom Warren, "Windows Phone Is Dead," Verge.com, January 28, 2016, http://www.theverge.com/2016/1/28/10864034/windows-phone-is-dead.

10. Quy Huy and Timo Vuori, "Who Killed Nokia? Nokia Did," *Salamander* magazine, January 28, 2016, http://alumnimagazine.insead.edu/who-killed-nokia-nokia-did/.

11. Mike Bland, "Turning Learning Up to 11: Transparent Internal Operations," 18F, January 4, 2016, https://18f.gsa.gov/2016/01/04/turning-learning-up-to-11-transparency/.

12. Jared M. Spool, "Fast Path to a Great UX—Increased Exposure Hours," User Interface Engineering, March 30, 2011, https://www.uie.com/articles/user_exposure_hours/.

13. Marvin Lange, interview, 2015.

14. Stephen Thomas Erlewine, AllMusic, http://www.allmusic.com/album/kind-of-blue-mw0000191710.

15. Stefon Harris, "There Are No Mistakes on the Bandstand," TED talk, November 2011, https://www.ted.com/talks/stefon_harris_there_are_no_mistakes_on_the_bandstand?language=en.

16. Julie Anixter and Sarah Miller Caldicott, "Midnight Lunch: How Thomas Edison Collaborated," Innovation Excellence, February 3, 2013, http://www.innovationexcellence.com/blog/2013/02/03/midnight-lunch-how-thomas-edison-collaborated/.

17. Rhys Newman and Luke Johnson, "No Dickheads! A Guide to Building Happy, Healthy, and Creative Teams," Medium, March 26, 2015, https://medium.com/@rhysys/no-dickheads-a-guide-to-building-happy-healthy-and-creative-teams-7e9b049fc57d#.dir4udkg9.

18. Eric Johnson, "Meet Shani Hilton, BuzzFeed's Newsmaker in Chief," Recode, January 21, 2016, http://recode.net/2016/01/21/meet-shani-hilton-buzzfeeds-newsmaker-in-chief/.

19. John Borthwick, "Tech Is Eating Media. Now What?" Medium, November 9, 2015, https://medium.com/@Borthwick/time-for-a-change-2be0 8d01d40.

20. Michael Calderone, "New York Times Eyes Ambitious Over-haul in Quest for 'Journalistic Dominance,'" *Huffington Post*, February 4, 2016, http://www.huffingtonpost.com/entry/new-york-times-overhaul_ us_56ae5e36e4b00b033aaf88d5.

21. David Gelles, "The Zappos Exodus Continues After a Radical Management Experiment," *New York Times Bits* blog, January 13, 2016, http://bits.blogs.nytimes.com/2016/01/13/after-a-radical-management-experiment-the-zappos-exodus-continues/.

Index

Index

Index

Index

Index

About the Authors

Jeff Gothelf is an author, speaker, and organizational designer. Over his nearly twenty years in digital products and services, he has worked to bring a customer-centric, evidence-based approach to product strategy, design, and leadership.

Josh Seiden is a designer, strategist, and coach. He has created award-winning products in Silicon Valley, built design teams on Wall Street, and taught modern product design and development methods across the globe.